A DICTIONARY OF INTERESTING & IMPORTANT DOGS

A DICTIONARY OF INTERESTING & IMPORTANT DOGS

PETER J. CONRADI

First published in the UK in 2019 by Short Books
an imprint of Octopus Publishing Group Ltd
Carmelite House, 50 Victoria Embankment
London, EC4Y 0DZ

www.octopusbooks.co.uk
www.shortbooks.co.uk

An Hachette UK Company
www.hachette.co.uk

This paperback edition published in 2021

10 9 8 7 6 5 4 3 2 1

A CIP catalogue record for this book is available
from the British Library.

ISBN 978-1-78072-517-8

Printed and bound in Great Britain by Clays Ltd, Elcograf S.p.A

This FSC® label means that materials used for the
product have been responsibly sourced

FSC www.fsc.org
MIX
Paper from responsible sources
FSC® C104740

CONTENTS

PREFACE

To Cloudy, Sky, Bradley and Max: four collies

We acquired Cloudy, the first in a succession of four collies, in 1987. A six-week-old, blue-eyed puppy little enough to hold on the palm of one hand, she was hiding in the stables with the rest of her litter when my partner Jim picked her up. She at once put her head trustingly against his chest, closing her eyes just as Jim closed his. Here was love at first sight. Cloudy reappears in this book under the entry 'Iris Murdoch's Pyrrhus and other dogs'. She was a blue-merle collie from a Radnorshire farm. Blue merles are genetically albino, and so have silver-and-white rather than black-and-white coats, and (often) blue rather than brown eyes. It is said that some Welsh Baptist farmers in the nineteenth century feared the blue merle's penetrating gaze, and would drown these pups soon after birth.

Cloudy grew up to be beautiful, affectionate, energetic and intelligent: a typical border collie. Immediately after a walk of twenty miles – once you factored in the additional distance she ran for the ball – she still tended to race a few times around the perimeter of our fields in

Wales, expressing sheer joy and the love of movement. Her propensity for hiding behind trees in Battersea Park before running athletically to catch and return balls attracted the memorable comment from one spectator: 'Well bugger me said the duchess'. We learned too late that we were over-exercising her. She was nearly fourteen when her daily dose of Metacam to alleviate arthritic pain caused kidney failure and we had to request the vet's help to see her off.

She understood a hundred or so words or commands, and would arrange herself with her bottom lowered to help us pick her up. She learned to push apart patio windows by moving her muzzle sideways, and once – after attentively watching me collect stones in a brook to create a rill – plunged her head under water to bring me stones herself. Her remarkable habit of barking angrily at the words 'Mrs Thatcher' got her photo and story on to the centre pages of the *Evening Standard*. Cloudy also knew how to wait in anticipation, understanding the future tense. When her 'auntie' was due to come and take her out for a walk, we could simply say 'Daphne, later!', and she'd go to the top of the stairs and wait for the sound of Daphne's car (and yes, she could distinguish the sounds different cars made).

Cloudy loved chasing airborne kites and skeetered about wildly, mirroring the movements she witnessed in the sky. This triggers a reflection on how incalculably different even dogs of the same breed can be. Kites so terrified her successor, a pure white collie called Sky, that on one occasion she ran a mile home across the South Circular Road and we lost her for two hours. Sky was independent-spirited as a princess and wilful to the point of recklessness, with a lifelong habit of finding plastic to chew until she finally and fatally perforated her gut. A week of unsuccessful surgery followed before the vet helped her on her way. We buried her in our orchard. She was just five.

Her brindled brother Bradley, acquired from the same litter, was the runt, and timorous to a fault. Even flies caused him to flee from a room, and he never outgrew a certain daffiness. He barked wildly at the sound made by the rotation of a salad spinner; and his habit of greeting people effusively prompted one friend to name him Sir Licksalot. When we dredged our pond of weed in Wales, he acted as foreman, issuing strange instructions, always pulling wildly on the rope in exactly the wrong direction. His character improved after his sister died, when he no longer had to compete for attention or affection; and he lived to be fourteen, when a cancer in his gut migrated to his lung.

His successor, our fourth and current collie, called Max, has a classic glossy black coat, with a white blaze down his muzzle, white ruff, white paws and white tip to his tail. And beautiful amber eyes. He invents games, like making believe that a stone is really a baby mouse, and squealing at it. Puppy-like, he enjoys frantically herding air bubbles in the brook or paddling his fleece manically between his rear legs before tossing it in the air. He loves chasing planes and will also try to round up swallows who look as if they are playing with him, hawking low for insects just above his head. He will inch his way under any low-slung bed to hide as if in a den. (When he lies down, his posture exactly recalls a cat's, with rear legs fully extended.)

Max – though like timid Bradley the runt of the litter – is as brave as a lion. Little seems to daunt him. True, he prefers Wales to London and used to throw up accordingly when our car reached the Cromwell Road. Once when he was very young we made the mistake of putting him in kennels, where he got no love or attention. And now he waits anxiously by any luggage he spots, lest he be forgotten or left behind when we travel. These habits apart, little frightens Max. He loves most human beings and, even as a pup, would wrap his front paws around strangers and try to hug them. He can balance magically on both front legs for half a second when he pees – a feat we have never before heard of; or on his rear legs for other purposes.

Each of these four very different collie dogs has enriched and transformed our lives. Loving them made me curious; and so this book is dedicated to all of them: to Cloudy, Sky, Bradley and Max.

INTRODUCTION: ON NOT WADING THROUGH TREACLE

'Without music life would be a mistake,' said the philosopher Nietzsche. But life, so it seems to me, might be hard without dogs too; and if I had the impossible task of choosing between letting go of music or letting go of dogs, I might conceivably choose to relinquish music, albeit with some anguish. It is wonderful to inhabit a world containing both.

How our love for dogs and theirs for us makes life bearable is the inspiration for this book, an anthology of interesting dogs in life and literature, and of dog-related prose and poetry that I enjoy.

The mutual love between man and dog frequently leads to myth-making, and not everything written about dogs deserves to be believed. We can, for example, read on the internet of an impressive dog named Delta, discovered during the excavations of Pompeii (or possibly Herculaneum) and preserved by the hardened volcanic ash. Delta was found hunched over a small boy, his master, apparently trying to save him from the disaster. 'A collar around his neck revealed not only the dog's name, Delta, and his master's (Servinus), but also that the faithful hound had saved the boy three times before, once from drowning, again from four robbers, and finally from a wolf set on attacking him at the sacred grove of Diana. Moreover, Delta's heroism lasted until the end: his corpse, frozen in time, will forever be protectively draped over the body of his beloved Servinus, a sort of living monument to devotion and fidelity.'

The difficulty is that this story is not authenticated anywhere and appears to be an early 'urban myth'. Nor is it by any means alone; there are many others like it. The tales of Gelert, Foxie and Greyfriars Bobby, all of which gain entries here, are each at least in part legends of canine loyalty that flatter and console us, sentimental fictions that endorse our pious belief in our central importance to the universe. Many such entries in this book stem from the nineteenth century, when the Victorians tended to beatify their dogs.

Perhaps for this reason Max Hastings, who clearly loves his own Labradors, has compared the experience of reading anthologies of writings about dogs to wading through treacle. His comment appears in his review of Carmela Ciuraru's wonderful *Dog Poems* (2003), an excellent anthology to which I owe the discovery of a dozen or so poems that are happily plundered here. Hastings observes that dogs, like Swift's horses in *Gulliver's Travels*, are often idealised as if they had 'all the virtues of Man without his Vices'.

This book attempts to be a little different. While the saccharine and sentimental can't wholly be avoided, the ironic, the unexpected and the provocative have their place too. So does the attempt to see the world from a dog's perspective rather than our own. And two recent books, one French, one American, give us hints as to how this might be done.

The Gallimard editor and writer Roger Grenier (1919-2017) published his unexpected bestseller *Les larmes d'Ulysse*, in 1998. Its English title is *The Difficulty of Being a Dog* and Grenier's English translator Alice Kaplan calls it 'a charming survey of writing about dogs through the ages'. Although only 130 pages long, Grenier's anthology seems much bigger. Its charm resides in its easy sweep, and the depth of reading, thinking and feeling that underlie its magisterial, lapidary shorthand.

'My book about dogs is an assembly of people I like,' Grenier boasts, accurately. He knew the great and the good and often shares first-hand anecdotes. After participating in the 1944 liberation of Paris, he joined Albert Camus at the newspaper *Combat* and indeed edited Camus's works after he died in 1960. The French existentialist author was a dog-lover himself; he wrote in his novel *The Fall*: 'I have a very old and very faithful attachment for dogs. I like them because they always forgive.'

At Gallimard, Grenier's office was next door to that of the writer Raymond Queneau, who brought his Tibetan terrier to work just as Grenier brought his St Germain pointer. Queneau's surname, Grenier tells us, derives from the Norman French dialect word for dog, related to the English 'kennel'.

Even when not writing about his own friends or acquaintances, Grenier manages to convey a sense of intimacy. He is clubby and knowing – whether he is writing about Aristotle (who recorded the different ways dogs and bitches piss), Kafka (addicted to self-accusation), Virginia Woolf (connoisseur of solitude) or Jack London. In just a few pages we can find apt and interesting anecdotes about dogs in relation to Paul Valéry, Sartre, Maeterlinck, Rilke, Balthus, Katherine Mansfield, Elizabeth von Arnim, Chesterton and Baudelaire.

Though we are tragically alone on this random planet, he shows us, our love of dogs and our uncanny (relative) ease of communication with them offer us a rare 'protection against life's insults, a defence against the world'. We can love dogs while despairing of humans. Grenier mentions Mme de Sévigné but does not repeat her trenchant observation '*Plus que je vois les hommes, plus que j'aime les chiens…*'.

This strange love-affair between species is not, he observes, without misunderstanding. Owners can be baffled when their pets roll around in excrement for camouflage and get themselves ready for hunting; while dogs spend much energy observing and decrypting the body-language and commands of their owners, commands that can carry a threat of punishment or even death. The mixed-breed terrier Nipper – who merits his own entry in this dictionary – cocks his head while staring into the HMV gramophone horn, trying to figure out where the noise is coming from: and as such is a potent symbol of the need for translation between dogs and men and of the ways in which dogs are obliged to live 'at the very limits of their nature... every minute carries its ration of anguish'.

The French sometimes refer to dogs as *bêtes de chagrin*, since they are short-lived animals and so provide us with a memento mori... They open our hearts and remind us of the hurt of living. They even open the hearts of tyrants. Napoleon – who declared that the deaths of millions left him cold – recorded the sight of a dog howling and licking his dead master's face on an Italian battlefield, his single most affecting memory. He was also forced to share Josephine's bed with her pug-dog Fortuné. Hitler loved dogs but – to test out the efficacy of his cyanide pill and make sure it would actually work – he had his physician administer one to his Alsatian bitch Blondi who died as a result.

Grenier is a source of esoteric knowledge: calling somebody a dog was an insult in both ancient Greek and Latin and the Romans called the letter 'L' the dog-letter as it sounded like a growl. Ulysses, after weeping at the death of his beloved hunting dog Argos, nonetheless goes on to use the word 'dogs' insultingly of Penelope's suitors. But Grenier is always willing to see the world from the dog's point of view, and this is unusual.

***

In her groundbreaking book *The Hidden Life of Dogs* (1994), which came out during the same decade as Grenier's and also quickly became a bestseller, Elizabeth M. Thomas poses some interesting questions about dog consciousness too. Do dogs have thoughts or feelings? Can a dog invent a custom or a game, weigh up two alternatives, or adopt a human mannerism? What do dogs want? A novelist as well as a scientist, Thomas writes that 'despite a vast array of publications on dogs, virtually nobody... had ever bothered to ask what dogs do when left to themselves'. Human vanity causes us to anthropomorphise and sentimentalise dogs: Thomas gives them back their own reality.

One day she started wondering about her two-year-old husky Misha, who had a habit of disappearing every evening on a secret errand of his own. What errand? Her book starts to resemble a detective story; and the mystery she is determined to solve concerns Misha's absences.

They are living in Cambridge, Massachusetts, a city of some 100,000 on the other side of the Charles river from Boston, and home to Harvard University. The perils of the city include dog-nappers then supplying the university's laboratories with animals for experimentation. Misha evades these, just as he evades traffic, poisonous bait and fights with other dogs. How? It is while mulling this question over that Thomas stumbles on her mission, one so simple-minded as to appear positively visionary. She sets out to discover how dogs behave when left to their own devices, without human intervention.

Her researches entail her trailing Misha and other dogs on her bicycle for two to three nights a week over a period of two years, during which she makes startling discoveries. Her dogs sometimes leave home for days, travelling more than 20 miles, returning with deer hair in their stools. She logs more than 100,000 hours of observation and finds that Misha's home range approximates to an astonishing 130 square miles, resembling that of wolves roaming in the wild. Misha's aim, she decides, is to circle other dogs.

As well as a passionate love of dogs, Thomas has a shocking and eccentric patience. She seems incapable of boredom and passes on this gift to us. Her fieldwork with wolves helps her. On Baffin island in high summer there is no darkness, and she was thus able on one occasion to watch a wolf – tired from hunting – sleeping for eighteen hours straight. 'After his first nine hours of motionless sleep, he raised his head, sighed, opened and shut his mouth to settle his tongue, and went back to sleep for a further nine hours'.

She displays the same patience at home, where she spent weeks lying on her elbows with her dogs in the enclosure they made for themselves when left alone. 'I've been to many places on the earth, to the Arctic, to the African savannah, yet wherever I went, I always travelled in my own bubble of primate energy, primate experience, and so never before or since have I felt as far removed from what seemed familiar as I felt with these dogs, by their den. Primates feel pure, flat immobility as boredom, but dogs feel it as peace.'

She records the lives of eleven large dogs – mainly German shepherds and huskies – five males and six females (including a dingo); and the birth of 22 pups, some on her bed. Her dogs are not pets. She makes no effort even to house-train them: the young dogs copy and learn from the older ones, and she is a shrewd and fascinating observer of doggy hierarchy. Their moral sense is made clear through an incident in which a tiny pug stops a much larger dog from terrorising some pet parakeets and mice.

Just as impressively, Thomas shows us how each canine is a complex individual. Particularly absorbing is her account of the 'romantic love' between Misha and his mate Maria, who remains monogamous even while on heat. She also tells an astonishing story of how her dogs, left wholly to their own devices, secretly dig a wolf-like den behind a woodpile. Its entrance is a tunnel, penetrating horizontally fifteen feet into the side of a hill and leading to a chamber three feet wide, two feet high and three feet deep. It provides a perfect climate of around 55 degrees Fahrenheit all year round. They never use it when a human being is present.

What, then, do dogs want? 'They want to belong, and they want each other.' This is popular science of a high order: Thomas tracks dogs into their own world, and in doing so has created a classic on a level with J.R. Ackerley's *My Dog Tulip*, which is beautifully observed, and a revelation to read. 'Like most people who hunger to know more about the lives of the animals,' she writes, 'I have always wanted to enter into the consciousness of a non-human creature. I would like to know what the world looks like to a dog, or sounds like or smells like: I would like to visit a dog's mind.'

A

ADVICE TO A DOG PAINTER

Happiest of the spaniel race,
Painter, with thy colours grace,
Draw his forehead large and high,
Draw his blue and humid eye;
Draw his neck, so smooth and round,
Little neck with ribands bound;
And the musely swelling breast
Where the Loves and Graces rest;
And the spreading, even back,
Soft, and sleek, and glossy black;
And the tail that gently twines,
Like the tendrils of the vines;
And the silky twisted hair,
Shadowing thick the velvet ear;
Velvet ears which, hanging low,
O'er the veiny temples flow.

Jonathan Swift (1667–1745)

ALEXANDER POPE AND HIS DOGS

Pope (1688–1744) was a great lover of dogs – dogs figure significantly in his imaginative universe and there are 100 references to them in his oeuvre. He was less sparing of people. Once called 'the wasp of Twickenham', he remains among the greatest satirical poets in English and his fierce critiques of prominent figures made him many enemies. At one point he deemed it necessary to carry pistols while walking his beloved Great Dane, Bounce, who also protected the diminutive poet (just four foot six inches in height).

In 1738, when Bounce sired pups, Pope offered one of them to Frederick, Prince of Wales, together with a collar engraved with perhaps his most famous satirical couplet:

> I am His Highness' dog at Kew
> Pray tell me, Sir: Whose dog are you?

These epigrammatic lines hint that every human being who reads them is either predatory, fawning or opportunistic, or a mixture of all three.

ARGOS

At the end of *The Odyssey*, after ten years fighting in Troy, followed by ten further years struggling to get home, Odysseus finally arrives back in Ithaca, his homeland. In his absence, greedy suitors have taken over his palace, competing to marry his wife Penelope and appropriate his wealth and estates. Odysseus, disguised as a beggar, plans to re-enter his house and spring a surprise attack on the suitors. His son Telemachus alone knows his true identity. As Odysseus approaches his home, he finds Argos lying mangy and neglected on a pile of cattle manure, infested with fleas, old and very tired. This is in sharp contrast to the dog Odysseus left behind. Argos was famous for his speed, strength and superior tracking skills.

No one else, not even Eumaeus, his lifelong servant and loyal friend, recognises Odysseus. Argos does so at once but, while he has just enough strength to drop his ears and wag his tail, he does not have enough to get up to greet his master. Odysseus passes by, unable to make a fuss of his beloved dog, as this would reveal who he really is, and he sheds a tear as he enters his hall, while Argos dies.

The simplicity of the relationship between Argos and Odysseus contrasts with the duplicity and deceit of the human world, and doubly emphasises the close links between man and dog. Is Argos's feat of memory believable? Our first dog, I remember, though highly intelligent, gave little sign of recognition when she ran into her own pups after five years. Yet the story of Argos and Odysseus is touching precisely because it stretches credulity: it bespeaks the strongest conceivable bonds already existing between man and dog nearly 3000 years ago.

Excerpt from *The Odyssey*

As they were speaking, a dog that had been lying asleep raised his head and pricked up his ears. This was Argos, whom Odysseus had bred before setting out for Troy, but he had never had any benefit from him. In the old days he used to be taken out by the young men when they went hunting wild goats, or deer, or hares, but now that his master was gone he was lying neglected on the heaps of mule and cow dung that lay in front of the stable doors waiting for the men to draw it away to fertilise the great estate and he was dirty and full of fleas. As soon as he saw Odysseus standing there, he dropped both his ears and wagged his tail, but could not get close up to his master. When Odysseus saw the dog on the other side of the yard, he dashed a tear from his eyes without Eumaeus seeing it, and said: 'Eumaeus, what a noble hound is that over yonder on the manure heap: his build is splendid; is he as fine a fellow as he looks, or is he only one of those dogs that come begging about a table, and are kept merely for show?'

'This dog,' answered Eumaeus, 'belonged to him who has died in a far country. If he were what he was when Odysseus left for Troy, he would soon show you what he could do. There was not a wild beast in the forest that could get away from him when he was once on its tracks. But now he has fallen on evil times, for his master is dead and gone, and the women take no care of him. Servants never do their work when their master's hand is no longer over them, for Zeus takes half the goodness out of a man when he makes a slave of him.'

So saying he entered the well-built mansion and made straight for the riotous suitors in the hall. But Argos passed into the darkness of death, now that he had fulfilled his destiny of faith and seen his master once more after twenty years.

ASHOKA

This Indian Buddhist emperor (c. 268 to 232 BCE) restricted the slaying of animals for food and created hospitals for animals, including dogs. The Mauryan Empire under Ashoka has been described as 'one of the very few instances in world history of a government treating its animals as citizens who are as deserving of its protection as the human residents'.

B

BITCH

In many languages 'bitch' or its equivalent is rarely used of a female dog: because it has been co-opted for humans, the word is thought insulting. Scott Fitzgerald in *The Great Gatsby* has fun with Myrtle's use of the genteelism 'lady-dog' instead. But the implied slur in this displacement of the word 'bitch' from dogs to women is itself unjust. It is true that a bitch can produce a litter sired by more than one male; and it is also true that dogs lack an incest taboo: a dog can mate with his daughter, a bitch with her son, though Elizabeth M. Thomas states the latter is much rarer. However, the interest of female dogs in sex is restricted to the period when they are on heat: once or twice (at most) a year. In this sense dogs, for most of the year, are far more sexually continent than human beings.

The recent naming of public promiscuous sex as 'dogging' is also inappropriate – if not insulting. This is not the only example of the use of the word 'dog' to demean or diminish; others include doggerel for lame poetry and dog Latin for a debased form of language. The French word *'canaille'* for riff-raff or rabble, coming as it does from the Latin word for dog, is similarly disobliging.

BLUEY, THE WORLD'S OLDEST DOG

Bluey – aka Bluey Les Hall – an Australian cattle dog owned by Les and Esma Hall, who managed a farm in Rochester in the state of Victoria, two hours north of Melbourne, lived from 7 June 1910 to 14 November 1939. Claims for dogs with even greater longevity exist, but are uncorroborated by paperwork. Bluey, at just under 30 years, is, according to *The Guinness World Records*, officially the world's oldest dog.

BOATSWAIN AND BYRON

According to Walter Scott, Byron loved his dogs very much: 'the companionship of a dog seemed to him almost as necessary as a hat or a stick. A man was not complete without a dog and a dog was scarcely complete without a man; Byron agreed with this'. Byron wrote 'Epitaph to a Dog' in 1808 in honour of his Newfoundland dog Boatswain, who had just died of rabies. When Boatswain contracted the disease, Byron reportedly nursed him without any fear of being bitten and infected. The poem is inscribed on Boatswain's tomb, which is larger than his master's, at Newstead Abbey, Byron's estate. The twelve memorial lines before the poem were written by Byron's friend John Hobhouse:

Near this Spot
are deposited the Remains of one
who possessed Beauty without Vanity,
Strength without Insolence,
Courage without Ferocity,
and all the virtues of Man without his Vices.

This praise, which would be unmeaning Flattery
if inscribed over human Ashes,
is but a just tribute to the Memory of
Boatswain, a Dog
who was born in Newfoundland May 1803
and died at Newstead Nov. 18th, 1808.

Epitaph to a Dog

When some proud Son of Man returns to Earth,
Unknown to Glory, but upheld by Birth,
The sculptor's art exhausts the pomp of woe,
And storied urns record who rests below.
When all is done, upon the Tomb is seen,
Not what he was, but what he should have been.
But the poor Dog, in life the firmest friend,
The first to welcome, foremost to defend,
Whose honest heart is still his Master's own,
Who labours, fights, lives, breathes for him alone,
Unhonoured falls, unnoticed all his worth,
Denied in heaven the Soul he held on earth –
While man, vain insect! hopes to be forgiven,
And claims himself a sole exclusive heaven.

Oh man! thou feeble tenant of an hour,
Debased by slavery, or corrupt by power –
Who knows thee well, must quit thee with disgust,
Degraded mass of animated dust!

Thy love is lust, thy friendship all a cheat,
Thy tongue hypocrisy, thy heart deceit!
By nature vile, ennobled but by name,
Each kindred brute might bid thee blush for shame.
Ye, who behold perchance this simple urn,
Pass on – it honours none you wish to mourn.
To mark a friend's remains these stones arise;
I never knew but one – and here he lies.

BUCK IN JACK LONDON'S *THE CALL OF THE WILD*

Buck, a large and powerful St Bernard/border collie cross is the hero of *The Call of the Wild* (1903). The story is divided into four parts. At the start, Buck experiences violence and struggles for survival; next, he proves himself leader of the pack; the third part brings him close to symbolic death and in the final part he undergoes rebirth. Like other epic heroes, he takes a journey, is transformed, and achieves an apotheosis. We experience the story through Buck's eyes and through his reflections:

> There he lay for the remainder of the weary night, nursing his wrath and wounded pride. He could not understand what it all meant. What did they want with him, these strange men? Why were they keeping him in this narrow crate?

Struck by this display of a dog philosophising, President Teddy Roosevelt famously called Jack London a 'nature-faker'. But as Roger Grenier points out, these are in fact the reactions of Jack London himself when he was locked up in the Erie County penitentiary in Buffalo for vagrancy in 1894. London made a speciality of books about marvellous dogs; he was also a passionate advocate of socialism and both workers' and animal rights.

He spent almost a year on the Klondike during the 1897 Gold Rush, and his experiences there helped feed his novel. He lived the whole winter in a temporary shelter reading Charles Darwin's *On the Origin of Species* and John Milton's *Paradise Lost*. Both are palpable influences, as is Kipling's *Jungle Book*. London contracted scurvy, common in the Arctic winters when fresh produce was unavailable; and when his gums began to swell – and he lost four front teeth – he decided to return to California, rafting 2000 miles down the Yukon River through portions of the wildest territory. He later said, 'It was in the Klondike I found myself.'

The Call of the Wild was serialised in the *Saturday Evening Post* in the summer of 1903 and published a month later in book form. It has never been out of print. As early as 1923, the story was adapted to film, and it has since seen several more cinematic adaptations.

C

THE CARPACCIO DOG

Ten minutes' walk from St Mark's Square in Venice, but mysteriously hidden away, is an unremarkable building with a simple façade called in Italian the *Scuola di San Giorgio degli Schiavoni* (roughly translatable as 'The School of St George of the Slavs'). The visitor finds herself in a small, dark, ground-floor room often empty of sightseers. With illumination switched on, nine panels spring unexpectedly into view: lucid yet domestic in scale and content, magically detailed, absolutely enchanting and wholly unlike the works of any other Great Master. These are the *Stories of the Patron Saints of the Scuola* by the painter Vittore Carpaccio, commissioned between 1502 and 1507.

The masterpiece in the series is the *Vision of St Augustine*, in which the saint is interrupted writing a letter to St Jerome, whom he hears supernaturally communicating news of his imminent death and ascent to heaven. The setting is an idealised version of the study of a cultured man of letters of the period versed in astronomy, sculpture and music. Bathed in strong light streaming in from the windows, each detail acquires a miraculous purity:

the desktop, the elegant chair, the library of books, the architectural ornamentation and the gilt bronze statue of the Saviour on the altar.

Then you notice the tiny dog seated to the left of the saint, looking up expectantly, patiently waiting for something to happen. Can this dog also hear that mysterious voice? Carpaccio's first thought was to include a cat, crouching, collared, resembling a weasel. He changed his mind and settled on a dog, whose breed nobody has ever been able to agree about: Ruskin in 1851 thought him a white spitz; the painter Molmenti considered him a lively spaniel; others – including the art critic Kenneth Clark – believe him to be 'a Maltese puppy'.

The great Welsh writer Jan Morris, whose last book (2014) is a celebration of Carpaccio, likes to consider him 'a dog of no particular breed, a tough urchin mongrel, cocky, feisty, and fun, rescued from the street perhaps by one saint or another, and cherished by multitudes down the centuries'. That Carpaccio was interested in dogs is also clear from his *Two Venetian Ladies on a Terrace*, in which one dog offers his paw to a lady holding a rope that a second happily tugs. Morris privileges the dog in the St Augustine picture, calling him simply 'the Carpaccio Dog'. This attentive dog is foregrounded, perfectly captured, superfluous to the story, and somehow joyous. He stands in here for all the dogs in art, from Titian and Rubens to Goya, Picasso and beyond.

CERBERUS

In July 1916, during the Battle of the Somme, the poet Robert Graves was hit by shrapnel from an exploding shell that pierced his chest and thigh. The army let Alfred Graves know that his son, a captain in the Royal Welch Fusiliers, had been killed and forwarded the family his personal belongings.

Among the many who read his obituary in *The Times* that month was Graves himself. For although certainly not in good health, he was still breathing, and would continue to do so for a long time. He was, however, gravely wounded and suffering undiagnosed shell-shock. The noise of a car backfiring would for a long time make him throw himself to the floor or send him running for cover. He was also obsessively fearful of a gas attack, to the point where any sudden, strong smell – even from flowers in a garden – set him 'trembling'. Although the army doctor gave him 'no chance', the poet later recorded that 'The joke contributed greatly to my recovery... The people with whom I had been on the worst terms during my life wrote the most enthusiastic condolences to my parents.'

He described the experience in a poem entitled

'Escape' which invokes the figure of Cerberus from Greek mythology, the dog who guards the entrance to the Underworld. His name probably derives from the Greek 'ker' and 'erobos' and translates roughly as 'Death-Daemon of the Dark'.

Why did a three-headed dog mark the boundary between life and death for the Ancients? Even the Egyptians had a canine-related god for the same borderline: Anubis. Scholars today debate whether Anubis's head is that of a jackal, coyote or wolf, but contemporary ancient Greek texts refer to Anubis as dog-headed. It is as if the company of dogs can mark not merely our lifetime, but also our passage to the next world.

Cerberus allowed everyone to enter, but seized those attempting to escape. He was variously represented with one, two or (usually) three heads, often with the tail of a snake or with snakes growing from his head or twined round his body. One of the ten tasks or labours imposed upon Heracles as penance for crimes he had committed was to fetch Cerberus from the Underworld, a favourite subject of ancient vase paintings. And Greek funeral custom then decreed that a man or woman be buried with a coin to bribe Charon, who ferries the dead across the river Styx into the Underworld, and food to distract Cerberus.

Graves in his poem bribes Cerberus with army jam drugged with morphine, so that he can escape death and return to life. (The death notice appeared on his 21st birthday; he lived to be 90.) Chatty and informal, the poem combines a conventional rhyme scheme with classical references: Lethe is the river of oblivion or forgetfulness; Lady Proserpine – a Latinisation of Persephone – is consort to the King of the Underworld.

Escape

…but I was dead, an hour or more.
I woke when I'd already passed the door
That Cerberus guards, and half-way down the road
To Lethe, as an old Greek signpost showed.
Above me, on my stretcher swinging by,
I saw new stars in the subterrene sky:
A Cross, a Rose in bloom, a Cage with bars,
And a barbed Arrow feathered in fine stars.
I felt the vapours of forgetfulness
Float in my nostrils. Oh, may Heaven bless
Dear Lady Proserpine, who saw me wake,
And, stooping over me, for Henna's sake
Cleared my poor buzzing head and sent me back
Breathless, with leaping heart along the track.
After me roared and clattered angry hosts
Of demons, heroes, and policeman-ghosts.
'Life! life! I can't be dead! I won't be dead!
Damned if I'll die for any one!' I said…

Cerberus stands and grins above me now,
Wearing three heads – lion, and lynx, and sow.
'Quick, a revolver! But my Webley's gone,

Stolen!... No bombs... no knife... The crowd swarms on,
Bellows, hurls stones... Not even a honeyed sop...
Nothing... Good Cerberus!... Good dog!... but stop!
Stay!... A great luminous thought... I do believe
There's still some morphia that I bought on leave.'
Then swiftly Cerberus' wide mouths I cram
With army biscuit smeared with ration jam;

And sleep lurks in the luscious plum and apple.
He crunches, swallows, stiffens, seems to grapple
With the all-powerful poppy... then a snore,
A crash; the beast blocks up the corridor
With monstrous hairy carcase, red and dun –
Too late! for I've sped through.
O Life! O Sun!

CONFESSIONS OF A GLUTTON

after i ate my dinner then i ate
part of a shoe
i found some archies by a bathroom pipe
and ate them too
i ate some glue
i ate a bone that had got nice and ripe
six weeks buried in the ground
i ate a little mousie that i found
i ate some sawdust from the cellar floor
it tasted sweet
i ate some outcast meat
and some roach paste by the pantry door
and then the missis had some folks to tea
nice folks who petted me
and so i ate
cakes from a plate
i ate some polish that they use
for boots and shoes
and then i went back to the missis swell tea party
i guess i must have eat too hearty
of something maybe cake

for then came the earthquake
you should have seen the missis face
and when the boss came in she said
no wonder that dog hangs his head
he knows hes a disgrace
i am a well intentioned little pup
but sometimes things come up
to get a little dog in bad
and now i feel so very very sad
but the boss said never mind old scout
time wears disgraces out

Don Marquis (1878–1937)

CRUFTS

Founded by dog biscuit salesman Charles Cruft in 1891, the inaugural event was billed as the 'First Great Terrier Show'. Five years later it was renamed 'Cruft's Greatest Dog Show' and opened up to all breeds. In 1991, Crufts was officially recognised by *The Guinness World Records* as the world's largest dog show. Now 27,000 dogs take part each year, with 160,000 human visitors attending. Crufts was televised by the BBC for half a century, an association that ended in 2008 when a BBC One documentary criticised breeding practices for compromising the health of pure-bred dogs. Statistically, the most likely breed to win the Best in Show crown is the cocker spaniel, which has come out on top seven times.

CYNICISM

The ancient Greeks invented cynicism, which comes from their word for 'dog', and equated it with philosophers who lived a carefree, vagabond, natural life, devoid of luxury, pride or malice. Since then, cynicism has gone downhill. Oscar Wilde quipped that the cynic knows the price of everything and the value of nothing. Today's cynic disbelieves in the possibility of altruism or good faith. Only the lowest motives count.

But it is heartening to know that a virtuous cynicism once believed that the purpose of life was to live in agreement with nature, rejecting conventional desires for wealth, power, sex and fame. Instead, cynics were – until a century or more after Christ – to lead a simple life free from all possessions, making a cult of indifference and, like dogs, eating and making love in public, going barefoot and sleeping out of doors.

D

DICKENS'S DIOGENES AND OTHER DOGS

In 1848, after he had finished writing *Dombey and Son,* Dickens suddenly realised he had forgotten to include Florence Dombey's dog Diogenes in the final round-up of characters. He sent an urgent message to his publisher via his friend John Forster, allocating the dog a mention. The single sentence '… an old dog is generally in their company' was accordingly inserted. This was not the only instance of Dickens's forgetfulness: Diogenes had started as a very large dog, dwindling into a smaller one; by Chapter 44 Dickens writes of his 'little shadow'.

At home, Dickens kept birds of various kinds, horses, poultry and cats, but loved dogs above all. They fascinated him and he wrote compellingly of them. His first was a shaggy white Havanese given him in America in 1842, whom he described as 'curling all over; and barking'. Dickens could name his dogs as quirkily as his characters: the toy-sized Havanese (under one foot at the shoulder) was first imposingly named Timber Doodle, then Snittle Timbery and finally plain Timber. Beryl Gray, in an excellent recent study, makes the point that, though Dickens mentions his wife Catherine in his letters 'far more often than Timber', he manages to convey the impression 'that the dog's company is more fun than hers'. This was despite Timber's chronic bowel problems during one journey across France in a carriage with five children, three nurses, a maid, a courier and Mr and Mrs Dickens. Catherine's habit of producing babies – nearly a dozen – was evidently less entertaining than Timber's willingness to jump over a stick or run into the corner of the room and stand on two legs, a habit Dickens later gave Dora's dog Jip in *David Copperfield*.

Dickens watched Timber's behaviour, trying to work out dog thought processes and psychology. He also took an interest in Timber's love life and on one occasion, when the dog was brought back from an arranged encounter in a state of 'disgrace and mortification',

having failed to perform, he had dark thoughts of killing him. At the advanced age of seven, poor Timber began to show interest in a 'drivelling, blear-eyed little tame rabbit of the female sex', for which Dickens unkindly and surely confusingly 'whopped' him. Timber, who may have preferred food to sex, died, aged twelve, in Boulogne in 1854.

There were other and much larger dogs once he had become the master of his country house Gad's Hill in Kent in 1857: Turk, a mastiff; Sultan, possibly an Irish bloodhound; Linda, a St Bernard (and four of her puppies, two to Turk, two to Sultan); and Don, a young black Newfoundland. The names – Turk, Sultan, Don – suggest their size and power. He walked with them when he was at Gad's Hill and they supported his new role as country squire. They were also helpful as guard dogs, intimidating passing tramps and prowlers on the nearby high road and protecting Dickens' sister-in-law and daughters when they went out walking. He boasted that they were 'the terror of the neighbourhood', a role Sultan overdid when – not chained and muzzled in the yard as usual like the other guard dogs – he savaged a young child, the little sister of one of the maids.

For this, Dickens first flogged Sultan and then, next morning, took him out and shot him, a procedure he describes in several letters: Sultan believed he was being led out for a treat.

Dickens enjoyed controlling his dogs: another, Bumble, was punished for running home ahead of his master by being dosed with castor oil. And one of Sultan's offspring was sent with the youngest Dickens boy, sixteen-year-old Plorn, to Australia. Neither Plorn nor the dog returned to England.

Dogs abound in the novels, from Bill Sikes's Bull's-Eye in *Oliver Twist*, with his scratched and torn face, kicked and cut by his master yet obstinately devoted to him, to Jip, the lapdog of *David Copperfield's* beloved and idiotic Dora Spenlow. There is also the terrible black dog that charges at David on his return from his mother's wedding – in some part an adjunct of the appalling Mr Murdstone. *Hard Times* has Merrylegs, the highly trained performing dog off-stage, while in *Little Dorrit,* Lion is the faithful dog belonging to the cruel and careless Henry Gowan.

One other real dog outside the fiction deserves mention: the white Pomeranian Dickens named Mrs Bouncer, a gift to his eldest daughter Mamie in 1859. Dickens's bond with Mrs Bouncer was so intense that he would dream of her every night when he was away from home, and years after his death, Mamie recollected how 'He had a peculiar voice and way of speaking for her, which she knew perfectly well and would respond to at once... To be stroked with a foot had great fascination for Mrs Bouncer ... and Charles Dickens would often take off his boot of an evening and sit stroking the little creature – while he read or smoked – for an hour together.' ('Charles Dickens at Home', *New York Times*, 6 April 1884).

Beryl Gray remarks of this anecdote: 'Among all the non-human creatures he maintained it is only Mrs

Bouncer who can be associated with domestic quietude; and of all the many portraits we have of Dickens, whether visual, written, or performed, this by his eldest daughter must be one of the most intimate and moving.'

DOG DREAMING

The paws twitch in a place of chasing
Where the whimper of this seeming-gentle creature
Rings out terrible, chasing tigers. The fields
Are licking like torches, full of running,
Laced odors, bones stalking, tushed leaps.
So little that is tamed, yet so much
That you would find deeply familiar there.
You are there often, your very eyes,
The unfathomable knowledge behind your face,
The mystery of your will, appraising.
Such carnage and triumph; standing there
Strange even to yourself, and loved, and only
A sleeping beast knows who you are.

W.S. Merwin (1927–2019)

DOGS IN THE ANTARCTIC

In 1911, Scott and Amundsen found themselves competing to reach the South Pole first. Amundsen famously won, while Scott and his team perished. In the 1920s, Amundsen was hurt to be called by some 'un-sportsman-like' and Scott has occasionally been criticised for want of leadership.

Be that it as it may, one of many factors that led to Amundsen's success was his use of dogs. He had gained experience with sledge dogs during an earlier trip across the Northwest Passage, where he learned from the Inuit how to use them and feed them, and what their strengths and weaknesses were. His plan with the dogs was to use them in the early part of the trip to pull heavy loads and to get up onto the Polar Plateau, then kill many of them and use them to feed the men and other dogs in the later part of the journey. This he duly fulfilled. Once up on the Polar Plateau, 24 dogs out of the 52 taken were killed, and eleven returned alive. The speed of the sledge dogs meant that longer periods of rest were possible and Amundsen's team actually gained weight during the journey to the pole, partly due to the extra food available from dogs killed en route.

Scott by contrast championed the exhausting process of man-hauling. He announced with questionable heroism: 'In my mind no journey ever made with dogs can approach the height of that fine conception which is realised when a party of men go forth to face hardships, dangers, and difficulties with their own unaided efforts, and by days and weeks of hard physical labour succeed in solving some problem of the great unknown. Surely in this case the conquest is more nobly and splendidly won.'

DOG NAMES

The naming of dogs changes from age to age according to fashion, so that to research dog names from a past epoch is to enter another country. One particularly rich and diverse period is the medieval era in England, especially as regards the naming of hunting dogs. Kathleen Walker-Meikle has uncovered many examples, including Sturdy, Whitefoot, Hardy, Jakke, Bo and Terri. And in Edward, Duke of York's book *The Master of Game,* in which he explains how dogs are to be used in hunting and taken care of, he lists 1100 dog names, including Amiable, Nameless, Clenche, Bragge, Ringwood and Holdfast. Anne Boleyn, second wife to King Henry VIII, called her dog Purkoy, a name derived from the French '*pourquoi*' because he was so inquisitive.

E

ENGLAND'S HAPPY DOGS

Dogs appear in a number of Stevie Smith's poems. In 'Archie and Tina' they are fond childhood playmates; while 'O Pug!' laments a dog suffering from insecurity. The first stanza of the poem that follows speaks for itself:

> O happy dogs of England
> Bark well as well you may
> If you lived anywhere else
> You would not be so gay.

F

FLUSH AND VIRGINIA WOOLF

Virginia Woolf's official account of the genesis of her novel *Flush* runs as follows: while she lay in her garden reading the Brownings' love letters, 'the figure of their dog made me laugh so I couldn't resist making him a Life'.

This is not the whole story. In autumn 1930, Leonard and Virginia Woolf went to the Queen's Theatre on Shaftesbury Avenue to see, early on in its run, Rudolf Besier's *The Barretts of Wimpole Street*. This play chronicles the pathological subjection of Elizabeth Barrett Browning both to her father – who was by strong implication incestuously possessive – and to invalidism. The play also shows her rescue by her future husband

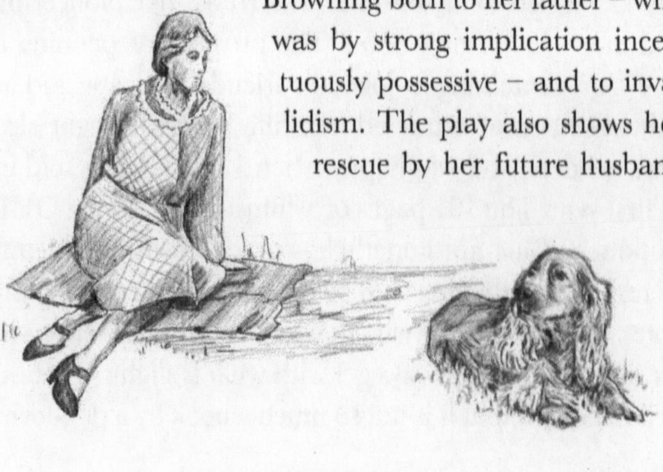

Robert Browning and their final flight to Italy. The part of Elizabeth's spaniel Flush was performed in the play by a dog called Tuppenny of Ware. He came on for all the curtain calls with Cedric Hardwicke and Gwen Ffrangcon-Davies. He was, after all, on stage throughout.

The dog's role in the play is to sleep in his basket or on the sofa, occasionally to be carried out for walks in the park. As bitter revenge for Elizabeth's elopement, her father orders that her dog be destroyed: only to learn in the play's last moments that she has already taken him to Italy. Meanwhile, her lisping cousin Bella says, 'Oh, wouldn't it be fwightfully intewesting if only dear Flush could speak!... You see, dear Flush is the only witness of all that goes on at Ba's weekly tête-à-tête with the handsomest poet in England. He – Flush, I mean – ought to know a wonderful lot about poetwy by this time!'

This conceit of a dog's possessing unique yet inaccessible testimony struck Woolf. She was that year emotionally exhausted after finishing *The Waves*, her pioneering and most challenging novel. The prospect of penning a *jeu d'esprit* containing in-jokes for friends as escape and as lightweight relief attracted her. She hoped it might also draw readers, and was happy when 19,000 copies sold in its first year. The 101 pages of whimsical text in the OUP edition of *Flush* are nonetheless preceded by 74 solemn pages of introduction and followed by portentous footnotes. It took her two years to write, and what is serious in the novel does not always gel with what is slight. Quentin Bell remarked that it is not so much a book by a dog-lover as 'a book by someone who would love to be a dog'.

Woolf used as a model her own pure-bred black cocker spaniel Pinka, who not only provided her with 'copy' but was photographed for the dust jacket and frontispiece of the first edition. She was a present from Vita Sackville-West (who bred spaniels) in 1926. Flush shares Pinka's high aristocratic breeding and pedigree but not the ability to perform the singular trick Woolf carefully taught Pinka and a whole succession of dogs: extinguishing with her paw the matches her owner used to light her cigarettes.

Woolf loved dogs yet felt equivocal about our ownership of them. Shag, her family's twelve-year-old Skye terrier, died in 1904 when she was 22; he had been chosen for his skill at killing rats, but also enjoyed biting people and fighting other dogs. Woolf wrote: 'There is some impertinence as well as some foolhardiness in the way in which we buy animals for so much gold and silver and call them ours… There is something, too, profane in the familiarity, half contemptuous, with which we treat our animals. We deliberately transplant a little bit of simple wild life and make it grow up beside ours, which is neither simple nor wild… How have we the impertinence to make these wild creatures forego their nature for ours, which at best they can but imitate?'

Perhaps these mixed feelings echoed in Woolf's depiction of Flush, a golden cocker. He is sympathetic towards human beings, and yet mystified by them. He has 'an even excessive appreciation of human emotions', can read signs that nobody else can see and gradually learns to read Elizabeth's feelings more closely than ever before… 'Every start she made… passed through him too'.

But his sense of affinity has limits. He, unlike his human owner, navigates through his nose, constantly cataloguing smells. 'The human nose is almost non-existent. The greatest poets… have smelt nothing but roses and dung… Yet it was in the world of smell that Flush mostly lived. Love was mostly smell; form and colour were smell; music and architecture, law, politics and science were smell. To him religion itself was smell… Italy… meant a succession of smells.' Perhaps for this reason he has 'never mastered the principles of human society'. Flush recalls Henry James's telegraphist in his 1898 novella *In the Cage*, struggling to decipher clues to her clients' personal lives from the cryptic cables they submit as she sits 'in the cage' at the post office.

Flush travels through six chapters, each providing a new and different *mise-en-scène*. He starts out in a working-man's cottage near Reading where he maps the odours of earth, flowers, leaves, bramble, hare and fox. His owner, the impoverished writer Mary Russell Mitford, soon delivers him to the Barrett household in Marylebone. Flush's spaniel ears, we are told, echo Elizabeth's fashionable ringlets: each perhaps completes what is dormant in the other.

Marylebone offers a new menu of smells: roasted joints, fowls, soups, cedarwood, sandalwood, mahogany, human scents, coal dust, followed by the invalid aromas of Elizabeth's back bedroom, including eau-de-cologne. Here he gets few airings or outings. He bonds with Elizabeth but experiences 'vast gaps in their understanding'. She feeds Flush treats off her plate, which satisfies her need to starve herself. But their intimacy is disturbed by the advent of Robert Browning. Both disliking and jealous of him, Flush twice attacks him.

In Chapter 4 Flush is kidnapped and Elizabeth blackmailed with the terrifying threat that his paws and head will be cut off and sent back unless she pays a ransom for his release. Dog theft was then commonplace and in real life Flush was stolen three times, adventures condensed in the novel into a single event. Confined somewhere in Whitechapel, Flush is desolate, thirsty and demeaned by his squalid, cruel and overcrowded surroundings. Elizabeth has to find £20 – roughly equivalent to £20,000 today – to get him back.

Finally he gets to Italy, where Florence's ubiquitous fleas cause him to have his coat shaved. Most dogs here are mongrels, and he relaxes about his own pedigree. When Elizabeth has a baby, he is at first disgusted by it but then learns to love it. Finally, he grows old and, just before he dies, Woolf quotes Elizabeth Barrett Browning's poem 'Flush or Faunus', the less mawkish of her two Flush poems, in which she chronicles her dog's absolute foreignness and hence his importance to her life journey. Faunus was the horned god of the Roman forest, plains and fields, a Latin equivalent to Pan, part-animal, part-human.

You see this dog. It was but yesterday
I mused, forgetful of his presence here,
Till thought on thought drew downward tear on tear;
When from the pillow, where wet-cheeked I lay,
A head, as hairy as Faunus, thrust its way
Right sudden against my face; two golden-clear
Large eyes astonished mine; a drooping ear
Did flap me on either cheek, to dry the spray!
I started first, as some Arcadian
Amazed by goatly god in twilight grove:
But as my bearded vision closelier ran
My tears off, I knew Flush, and rose above
Surprise and sadness; thanking the true Pan,
Who, by low creatures, leads to heights of love.

Flush died peacefully in summer 1854 and is buried in a cellar beneath Casa Guidi, the Brownings' home in Florence. Pinka died of an unexplained fit, aged only eight, while Virginia and Leonard Woolf were away on holiday abroad, in 1935. She wrote in grief to a friend: '...a dog represents the private side of life, the play side' and confided to her diary that part of her life was buried in the orchard.

FOXIE AND ROMANTICISM

In April 1805, a 20-year-old painter called Charles Gough disappeared on Helvellyn in the Lake District. He had set out on his hike accompanied by his bitch Foxie, according to some a spaniel, and to others an Irish terrier. Foxie has for two centuries been celebrated as the heroine of Gough's story – among the most gallant and iconic of all dogs – and it is no fault of hers if there are serious grounds for questioning the layers of myth and legend that surround her memory.

In July of the same year – three months after Gough disappeared – a shepherd heard a dog barking near Red Tarn and went to investigate. He soon found Gough's skeleton. People visited the scene and collected Gough's remains and some of his belongings, including fishing tackle, his hat (split in two), a gold watch, one silver pencil and two Claude glasses, those blackened pocket mirrors used in the heyday of Romanticism to frame picturesque views. Foxie was still in attendance, with one weakly puppy to whom she had given birth in the furze nearby. As a dog's pregnancy is reckoned at 58–68 days, Foxie was probably newly pregnant when Gough's accident happened. This pup died shortly after.

Gough is more famous for his death than for anything achieved in life. He seems to have been fashionably melancholic, and possessions found near Red Tarn include a notebook in which he had recorded epitaphs from gravestones in a country churchyard. A water-colourist, his picturesque landscapes depict Welsh mountain valleys, waterfalls and woods. He had been contracted by a local artist to copy drawings. Gough was soon celebrated as a martyr to the Romantic ideal, and Foxie feted for her attachment and fidelity to her long-dead master. Wordsworth and Sir Walter Scott wrote poems about her; Francis Danby and Edwin Landseer painted the scene. In 1890, a memorial stone to Gough was erected on Helvellyn, quoting part of Wordsworth's poem 'Fidelity'. And Foxie was both prototype and model for later legends of doggy faithfulness such as Greyfriars Bobby.

If Gough's absence went at first unremarked, this may have been because he was a solitary figure or – as we might say nowadays – a loner. Helvellyn's Striding Edge is among the most famous, vertiginous and dangerous of all mountain ridge walks – for an alarming recent video of the walk see either 'Helvellyn via Striding Edge' or 'Walking Striding Edge, Helvellyn' on YouTube. But Gough had acquired a reputation for taking serious risks: the abolitionist Thomas Clarkson (1760–1846) after meeting Gough reported that he was a 'venturesome person whose headstrong nature had caused the local shepherds alarm'. This may help explain why he attempted the perilous ascent of Helvellyn on his own, without a guide. A volunteer in the local militia had agreed to accompany Gough but turned out on the day in question to be busy on parade: Britain was, after all, at war with France and 1805 the year of Trafalgar…

Later that year, Wordsworth, who lived five miles away in Grasmere, took his visitors Sir Walter Scott and the chemist Humphry Davy on pilgrimage to the spot where Gough had died. Scott recorded 'enthusiastic delight' about this visit and soon penned his lyric poem 'Helvellyn', containing the lines:

> … faithful in death, his mute favourite attended,
> The much-loved remains of her master defended,
> And chased the hill-fox and the raven away.

One unlikely theory about how Gough was reduced within a matter of weeks to a pile of bones was that he had been devoured by ravens. Scott hymns Foxie as patient, loyal and semi-human in her desire to keep Gough's body intact. He soon moves on to further melodrama and pathos:

> How long didst thou think that his silence was slumber?
> When the wind waved his garment, how oft didst thou start?
> How many long days and long weeks didst thou number,
> Ere he faded before thee, the friend of thy heart?
> And, oh! was it meet, that – no requiem read o'er him,

No mother to weep, and no friend to deplore him,
And thou, little guardian, alone stretched before him –
Unhonoured the pilgrim from life should depart?

Wordsworth's poem 'Fidelity' mines a similar vein of feeling:

Yes, proof was plain that, since the day
When this ill-fated Traveller died,
The Dog had watched about the spot,
Or by his master's side:
How nourished here through such long time
He knows, who gave that love sublime;
And gave that strength of feeling, great
Above all human estimate!

Wordsworth wonders how Foxie herself survived. Since the dog embodies natural virtues we human beings have lost, he speculates that she was kept going by divine sustenance or 'love sublime'. By contrast, a local Carlisle newspaper, in a tone of high indignation and moral shock, pointed out that Foxie's survival over three months and the dramatic state of Gough's remains – reduced to a skeleton within a mere twelve weeks – both point to the strong likelihood that she had been systematically eating her master. This – being a view unflattering to Romantic sensibility – was quietly ignored and forgotten. Yet no diet of rabbits was available to keep Foxie alive, nor was she strong enough to nurse her own puppy. And since human beings in extremity similarly resort to cannibalism, what is more likely than that a dog should turn to the nearest – and only – available source of food? Tales of dogs eating men are as old as Homer. This need not wholly undermine or contradict the tale of Foxie's fidelity, but it reminds us how anthropocentric – or selfish – our view of dogs has long been.

Wordsworth (unlike Scott) refers to Foxie as 'He' ('his master's side'), insufficiently interested in Foxie to notice that she is a bitch. It is not until J.R. Ackerley that we start to see the world from the dog's point of view, rather than our own. Meanwhile, Landseer painted Foxie in 1829 in an affecting vignette entitled 'Attachment', which shows a spaniel heart-breakingly keeping vigil over her owner's face, cold and white in death, thus starting a sub-genre of sentimental dog paintings – admired and praised by Ruskin – that has proven durable.

G

GEIST'S GRAVE

Matthew Arnold (1822–88), cultural critic, schools inspector and poet, wrote a number of animal elegies, including a laborious one for his canary ('Poor Mathias'), and another to his dachshund Kaiser, the last poem he completed before his death. The best of them is the ode that follows, written to his dog Geist (German for spirit or mind) who died aged four. Stanza 4's reference to Virgil alludes to the famous line in the *Aeneid*: 'there are tears in the heart of things; and men's affairs touch the heart'. Arnold excels at pathos, which in his best-known poem 'Dover Beach' he calls 'the eternal note of sadness'. 'Geist's Grave' is touching, tender, emotional and, of course, thoroughly anthropomorphic. He emphasises the fact that Geist was both loving and loved, recalling the spot where the animal was known to play. The beloved pet was also a devoted friend.

FOUR years! – and didst thou stay above
The ground, which hides thee now, but four?
And all that life, and all that love,
Were crowded, Geist! into no more?

Only four years those winning ways,
Which make me for thy presence yearn,
Call'd us to pet thee or to praise,
Dear little friend! at every turn?

That loving heart, that patient soul,
Had they indeed no longer span,
To run their course, and reach their goal,
And read their homily to man?

That liquid, melancholy eye,
From whose pathetic, soul-fed springs
Seem'd urging the Virgilian cry,
The sense of tears in mortal things –

That steadfast, mournful strain, consol'd
By spirits gloriously gay,
And temper of heroic mould –
What, was four years their whole short day?

Yes, only four! – and not the course
Of all the centuries yet to come,
And not the infinite resource
Of Nature, with her countless sum

Of figures, with her fulness vast
Of new creation evermore,
Can ever quite repeat the past,
Or just thy little self restore.

Stern law of every mortal lot!
Which man, proud man, finds hard to bear,
And builds himself I know not what
Of second life I know not where.

But thou, when struck thine hour to go,
On us, who stood despondent by,
A meek last glance of love didst throw,
And humbly lay thee down to die.

Yet would we keep thee in our heart –
Would fix our favorite on the scene,
Nor let thee utterly depart
And be as if thou ne'er hadst been.

And so there rise these lines of verse
On lips that rarely form them now;
While to each other we rehearse:
Such ways, such arts, such looks hadst thou!

We stroke thy broad brown paws again,
We bid thee to thy vacant chair,
We greet thee by the window-pane,
We hear thy scuffle on the stair.

We see the flaps of thy large ears
Quick rais'd to ask which way we go;
Crossing the frozen lake, appears
Thy small black figure on the snow!

Nor to us only art thou dear
Who mourn thee in thine English home;
Thou hast thine absent master's tear,
Dropp'd by the far Australian foam.

Thy memory lasts both here and there,
And thou shalt live as long as we.
And after that – thou dost not care!
In us was all the world to thee.

Yet, fondly zealous for thy fame,
Even to a date beyond our own
We strive to carry down thy name,
By mounded turf, and graven stone.

We lay thee, close within our reach,
Here, where the grass is smooth and warm,
Between the holly and the beech,
Where oft we watch'd thy couchant form,

Asleep, yet lending half an ear
To travellers on the Portsmouth road –
There build we thee, O guardian dear,
Mark'd with a stone, thy last abode!

Then some, who through this garden pass,
When we too, like thyself, are clay,
Shall see thy grave upon the grass,
And stop before the stone, and say:

People who lived here long ago
Did by this stone, it seems, intend
To name for future times to know
The dachs-hound, Geist, their little friend.

GELERT

Llywelyn Fawr or Prince Llywelyn the Great (c 1173–1240) was married to a daughter of Plantagenet King John and fought and dominated Wales for 45 years. The story of his favourite wolfhound Gelert, a gift from King John, must rank as one of Wales's great legends. The tale runs that Llywelyn comes home to find his son's cradle overturned and Gelert bloodied. He slays his faithful dog, only to discover a dead wolf Gelert had defended the child against. The dog's gore resulted from his struggle with the wolf, and the child had survived beneath the upturned cradle.

In 1793, a man called David Pritchard came to live in Beddgelert as landlord of the Royal Goat Inn. He adapted the story of the brave dog to fit the village, and benefit his trade at the inn. Some version of the same legend survives across many cultures: for example in Malaysia and Liguria, and also in India where the story features a pet mongoose and a snake. Gelert's purported grave still attracts visitors every year.

GREYFRIARS BOBBY

Greyfriars Bobby is surely the most famous dog in Scotland, and arguably one of the best-known dogs in the world. His life story has inspired two statues, Walt Disney's 1961 hit film, a second film in 2006, a stream of books and articles, and the name of a pub. The best-known version of the story is that Bobby belonged to John Gray, a night watchman working for the Edinburgh City Police. When John Gray died of TB in 1858 he was buried in Greyfriars Kirkyard in Edinburgh Old Town. Bobby then became known locally for spending the rest of his life – a further fourteen years – sitting faithfully on his master's grave, a vigil interrupted only when he left for his midday meal at Mr John Traill's restaurant (6 Greyfriars' Place) – announced by the sound of the time gun which actually fires at one o'clock.

The year after Bobby's death in 1872, the noted philanthropist Angela Burdett-Coutts, who was charmed by his story, commissioned a commemorative drinking fountain topped with Bobby's statue from the sculptor William Brodie, to go opposite the entrance to the churchyard and bearing the legend: 'A tribute to the affectionate fidelity of Greyfriars Bobby. In 1858 this faithful dog followed the remains of his master to Greyfriars Churchyard and lingered near the spot until his death in 1872.'

Embellishments to this legend started during Bobby's life time and continue today. In 1867, a new bye-law allegedly required all dogs to be licensed in the city or to be 'put out of the way': i.e. killed with an oral dose of prussic acid/cyanide. The dog tax collectors then wanted to recover fees from dog-owners, and if no owner for Bobby could be found, he would be destroyed. Edinburgh's Lord Provost Sir William Chambers decided to pay Bobby's licence and award him the Freedom of the City, presenting him with a collar with a brass inscription, 'Greyfriars Bobby from the Lord Provost 1867 licensed', which can be seen at the Edinburgh Museum.

On 27 April the same year, the *Spectator* reported that Bobby was finding the pressures of fame too much and beginning to presume himself 'superior to our human world'. Not only was he showing attachment to a master 'whom he can no longer see', but he was showing 'contempt and annoyance' with his sudden popularity. On a regular basis crowds would gather at the entrance of the kirkyard waiting for the one o'clock gun that would signal the appearance of Bobby as he left the grave for his midday meal. It seemed this audience with their 'admiring pats' stopped the dog from being able to concentrate on his dinner routine and his graveside vigil.

The *Spectator* concluded by addressing the question of whether dogs have souls: 'Surely that dog is as immortal as the invisible master he still loves?' A journalist on the *Scotsman*, meanwhile, claimed that Bobby was 'a Sabbath observer – at least to this extent, that he knows that the place of refreshment at which he gets his dinner on week-days is closed on Sunday; and he is sagacious enough to provide for this contingency by saving during the week odd scraps of food, which he hides beneath a tombstone adjoining the grave over which he keeps watch and ward.'

One year later, a letter from an Edinburgh resident to the *Scotsman* stated that news of Bobby had travelled far beyond the Tweed: a lady in Leamington had offered to subscribe for a kennel, 'to be placed over the grave so faithfully watched by the poor dog, to protect him from cold and rain'.

After Bobby's death, his legend grew further. In 1889, Edinburgh Town Council received a proposal, from a Mr and Mrs Slatter of Tunbridge Wells, to erect a monument of Sicilian marble to 'Greyfriars Bobby' in the churchyard, to mark the spot where he was buried. Hundreds of Kent children had given their pennies to fund the proposal. But not everyone was convinced. According to the *Pall Mall Gazette* (in an article entitled 'Playing Havoc With A Pathetic Story'), a Mr Gillies told the assembly the story of Bobby was 'a penny-a-liner's romance' and further questioned the moral decency of erecting a monument to a dog in a churchyard. Following Mr Gillies' statement, the *Edinburgh Evening News* ran a sombre editorial after doing their own research and resolved 'more or less conclusively' that evidence showed 'Greyfriars Bobby' to be a myth. The *Evening News* was not the first paper to try to pick holes in the Bobby story. Nearly two decades earlier in November 1871, the *Glasgow Daily Herald* had published an exposé of the hoax surrounding the shaggy dog tale. The writer explained he wouldn't have been bothered to give the true story, except that the 'benevolence of a noble lady [Burdett-Coutts] has been turned into improper channels, and a good-humoured joke has been dignified into something like a sentimental truth'.

None of this stopped another story popping up a little later, to the effect that special permission had been given to open John Gray's grave to allow his faithful companion to be interred with him. Meanwhile, Bobby's fame spread abroad. In 1915, a Mr and Mrs Howell Reed of Boston, Massachusetts, paid for a stone to mark John Gray's grave, with the inscription: 'Erected by American lovers of Bobby'. Then in 1981, another monument in red granite was erected close to Bobby's grave by the Dog Aid Society of Scotland and unveiled by the Duke of Gloucester. Its inscription reads: 'Greyfriars Bobby – Died 14 January 1872 – Aged 16 years – Let his loyalty and devotion be a lesson to us all.' Over recent decades this last monument has morphed into a shrine, with sticks left there for Bobby's spirit to run after and fetch, together with dog toys and flowers.

What are we to make of all this? By now the reliability of Greyfriars Bobby's story has been challenged many times. Even in November 1869, one councillor, Baillie Miller, told Edinburgh Town Council that 'the whole story about "Bobby" is a downright fabrication'. And Jan Bondeson, senior lecturer at Cardiff University – after spending years reviewing contemporary archives and eyewitness accounts – advances the view in a recent book that fundamental facts about the dog and his loyalty are all wrong.

Bondeson states as background that, in nineteenth-century Europe, there are over 60 documented accounts of churchyard or cemetery dogs. These were strays, fed by visitors and curators to the point that the dogs made the graveyards their home; the pious belief that they were waiting by a grave helped ensure that these dogs were looked after. Bondeson claims that after an article about Bobby appeared in the *Scotsman*, visitor numbers increased, creating a commercial benefit for the local community.

Bondeson believes Bobby never had an owner and that the original Bobby was a stray who wandered into nearby Heriot's Hospital before being taken to the graveyard and kept there with bribes of food. Indeed, a one-time gardener at Heriot's Hospital stated that Bobby was actually 'put' in the graveyard against his will (he was happier in the hospital garden) and then the caretaker of the graveyard kept chasing him out into the street. Eventually, according to Bondeson's thesis, the animal-loving gentleman who lived at the graveyard gate fed Bobby and an attachment grew. Bobby was also known to spend nights with another gentleman in Candlemaker Row, lying at his feet. It was said that Bobby never liked any 'working man' (as opposed to a gentleman), which also mitigated against the likelihood of his belonging to a poor man such as John Gray, who is sometimes – as in the Disney film – a farmer and in other versions a gardener turned night watchman.

Dr Bondeson believes the story was fabricated by James Brown, curator of the cemetery, and John Traill, who owned a nearby restaurant. Many donated money to the kind-hearted Mr Brown for taking care of Bobby and others dined in the next-door restaurant owned by Mr Traill. Thus the 140-year-old story was a publicity stunt drummed up by local businessmen to attract custom to their corner of Edinburgh. Dr Bondeson insists pictures and portraits of the dog, as well as contemporary accounts, show that the original Bobby died in May or June 1867. He believes it likely that Brown and Traill then substituted a similar dog, a Skye terrier, for the original terrier mongrel, to keep exploiting Bobby's fame.

Bondeson nonetheless adds: 'It won't ever be possible to debunk the story of Greyfriars Bobby – he's a living legend, the most faithful dog in the world, and bigger than all of us.' Stories about the loyalty of dogs flatter us, but are not entirely fables. Bobby's story is echoed by that of Hachikō in Japan (1923–35), who waited for his owner's return after his sudden death from a cerebral haemorrhage, appearing at precisely the time that his train was due at the station every day for nine years, nine months and fifteen days. The Italian dog Fido, for fourteen years after his rescuer and master was killed in an Allied air raid in 1943 until the day of his death, went daily to the bus stop, watching and waiting in vain for Carlo Soriani to get off the bus. And Shep from Fort Benton, Montana, USA, is believed to have watched as his deceased master's coffin was loaded onto a departing train one day in 1936 and then remained at the station, waiting for him to return for the next five and a half years, until he was killed by an incoming train in 1942.

H

THE HAIRY DOG

My dog's so furry I've not seen
His face for years and years;
His eyes are buried out of sight,
I only guess his ears.

When people ask me for his breed,
I do not know or care;
He has the beauty of them all
Hidden beneath his hair

Herbert Asquith (1881–1947)

HENRY VIII AND HIS DOGS

If you had to belong to Henry VIII, being an animal might have been safer than being a wife. By all accounts, he loved animals and kept ferrets, hawks, falcons and numerous other birds; the windows at Hampton Court are said to have been surrounded by cages containing canaries and nightingales. He also owned dozens of dogs and – after his death – more than 60 dog leashes were found in his wardrobe.

HOPE

At the foot of the stairs
My dog sits;
In his body
Out of his wits.

On the other side
Of the shut front door
There's a female dog
He's nervous for.

She's the whole size
Of his mind – immense.
Hope ruling him
Past sense.

William Dickey (1923–97)

THE HUMAN CONDITION

Some way into J.G.Farrell's fine novel *The Singapore Grip* (1978), set during the collapse of Singapore in 1942, Major Brendan Archer finds an elderly and decrepit King Charles spaniel tethered to his gatepost, together with five dollars and a badly written note urging the major 'as a lover of dogs' to have this one destroyed. The dog's coat, under attack from some kind of worm, is in some patches bald, in others matted and filthy. His tail hangs out at a drunken angle and it has been liberally coated with a substance resembling axle grease. A friend of the major's nicknames the dog 'The Human Condition': a simple and satisfying black joke about the dire processes of history. The major, who is both absent-minded and busy, keeps forgetting to take the dog to the vet's, and in the chaos and panic attending the Japanese takeover the Human Condition is last observed sneaking onto a boat immediately before the gangplank is raised, to escape the doomed city. The ship's captain, it is implied, will now take the Human Condition under his care.

I

IRIS MURDOCH'S PYRRHUS AND OTHER DOGS

The qualities of character displayed by a dog called Pyrrhus in Iris Murdoch's novel *An Accidental Man* add up to an indictment of the human race. A marvellous passage depicts Pyrrhus's equal dependence on and fear of us. We are painted as bottomlessly treacherous, shallow and given to pointless, uncontrollable rages. Dogs by contrast, are noble, innocent, generous and loyal.

> Pyrrhus, a large black Labrador, rescued, not for the first time, from the Battersea Dogs' Home, looked up anxiously from his place by the stove and wagged his tail. Pyrrhus's lot had always been cast with couples who fought and parted, abandoning him on motorways, on lonely moors, on city street corners. He had been called Sammy and then Raffles and then Bobo. He had only just learned his new name. He had been happy for a while in the snug cottage and the rabbitty wood with his new humans. Now perhaps it was all starting up all over again. He heard the familiar sounds of dispute, the cries, the tears, and he wagged his tail with entreaty. A virtuous affec-

> tionate nature and the generous nobility of his race had preserved him from neurosis despite his sufferings. He had not a scrap of spite in his temperament. He thought of anger as a disease of the human race and as a dread sign for himself.

His owners Charlotte and Mitzi quarrel about his future until Charlotte sheds 'defeated tears, and her tears were already like those of married people who love each other, cannot stand each other, and know that they can never now have any other destiny'. Small wonder that in two other Murdoch novels characters debate whether the predisposition of dogs to love us humans is a sign of innate intelligence or – given the pusillanimity of the human race – a sign of rank stupidity. That this love is given easily is attested by Nick in *The Bell* when he compares humans and dogs by pointing out that 'At least a dog can be trained to love you'. Dogs can also manifest the quality of attention that Murdoch so profoundly valued. In her 1982 Gifford lectures, she cited the great Austrian poet Rilke's praise for the painter Cezanne for attending to his subject matter, not as a human being watches, but as a dog watches, i.e. with devout intensity.

It is sometimes inaccurately thought that Iris Murdoch was a cat-lover: the author's photo on an inside flap of *The Unicorn* in 1963 shows her holding a white cat. But this animal belonged to her friend and photographer, Janet Stone, who requested that pose. Murdoch loved dogs and in her fiction celebrated many, starting with Mars in her first novel *Under the Net* (1954), the big film-star Alsatian kidnapped by the narrator Jake for purposes of extortion. Walking by the Seine in Paris, Jake notes in passing the joy all dog-owners feel, watching their animals swim.

The originals of Murdoch's fictional dogs often belonged to friends. Tadg in *The Unicorn* was based on John and Patsy Grigg's golden Labrador Crumpet and given a moving last scene, when he runs towards the horizon to be with Dennis, whom he loves. Zed in *The Philosopher's Pupil* was based on Diana Avebury's three-legged, shrilly barking papillon, Zelda. Murdoch said that she would be happily 'enslaved' [sic] to any dog she owned and regretted that – having so many other commitments – she could never be a dog-owner herself.

She certainly borrowed from life in her novels. After I learned in yoga classes how to stand on my head, one day in 1984, having lunch in the upstairs room at Dino's restaurant, empty apart from us, I offered to show her on the spot. She tensed up a little, and I desisted, but the episode was incorporated into *The Good Apprentice*, which was published the next year. Similarly, when in 1987 my partner and I acquired Cloudy, a blue-merle border collie with a silvery coat and blue eyes, Murdoch took a keen interest; and when we confessed to being in love with her, she commented that we 'seemed to have exactly the right attitude', adding that she 'should very much like to meet that beast'.

Murdoch was soon writing our collie into *The Green Knight*, where she appears as 'Anax', a soubriquet, she explained, for Apollo. This was her last successful novel, bearing comparison with the late romances of Shakespeare; poised and fantastical, it was a myth about redemption and an extraordinarily achieved mixture of joy and pain. She wanted carefully to check the dog's appearance and so gave me a salad lunch at home in Oxford while Cloudy spent a happy time feasting on the many scraps of old food to be found lying under the kitchen table. Murdoch was excited by the adventures she was devising for Anax, not all of which got into the published book. On reading a proof copy, we wrote facetiously as if from the dog proposing some editorial changes, which she duly made, the dog evidently carrying greater weight than the editor Jeremy Lewis at Chatto, whose corrections to an earlier novel she emphatically rejected.

We picked up our dog to cuddle her, and this got into the novel in the scene where Bellamy and his dog are reunited. So did our discovery that Cloudy liked drinking milk. When I enquired as to whether she had intended an identification between us and Bellamy James – a self-deluded ascetic who picks up Anax – she fiercely rebutted it in her usual quixotic fashion.

J

JUDY – NAVY POW DOG

Future generations will surely gape at the conceit that causes us to 'reward animals for their gallantry', enlisting members of the animal kingdom into our wars and killing zones before recompensing them for loyalty to 'our' side. Michael Morpurgo's *War Horse* educated us about the cost to other creatures of our blind and deadly anthropocentrism. So it's perhaps unsettling to read about an American organisation called the Marshall Legacy Institute that in 1999 launched the Mine Detection Dog Partnership Program (MDDPP).

The MDDPP website abounds in facts and figures. It has delivered over 900 mine detection dogs to 24 affected countries where they have searched more than 47 million square metres of land. The dogs are trained for three to five months in Texas or in Bosnia-Herzegovina to scent landmines and sit still, stay safe and alert a human partner to mark the spot. The mine is then removed or destroyed. Dogs' detection skills, agility and size – we are told – make them versatile and valuable partners. 'When a dog detects a mine, the handler praises and rewards the dog, usually with a ball or a toy. This makes the work fun for the dog, which motivates them to continue.' So that's alright then.

There is no mention of dog casualties and it is clear that this programme saves human lives and reclaims productive land. So perhaps some more formal gratitude to dogs is appropriate here; something like the gratitude institutionalised in 1943 by Maria Dickin when she started a prize in her name – commonly known as the 'animal VC' – to reward outstanding acts of bravery by animals serving with the armed forces. It is hard to read about this without mixed emotions (unease, amusement, incredulity...). In December 1943, three pigeons were thanked for contributing to the recovery of RAF air crew from ditched aircraft; while the most recent animal cited is a Belgian Malinois who served in Afghanistan in 2012. Over 70 years, the Dickin Medal has been awarded 70 times, and one honorary award was made in 2014 'to all the animals that served in WW1'. Perhaps the spirits of the eight million horses slaughtered during that holocaust were duly placated.

Among notable early recipients was Judy (1936–50), a highly intelligent white-and-liver English pointer. 'For magnificent courage and endurance in Japanese prison camps which helped maintain morale among her fellow prisoners,' reads her citation 'and also for saving many lives through her intelligence and watchfulness.' Lengthy Wikipedia entries and at least one book have been written about her career.

We discover from these that she was born in Shanghai,

where as a puppy she learned to sense and to bark at enemy planes long before they physically appeared or could be detected by human beings. This sixth sense saved hundreds of lives: Judy not only barked to warn of enemy bombers before they appeared: she reputedly also used canine cunning to stop Japanese guards killing POWs.

Judy was adopted as a ship's mascot first on HMS *Gnat*, then on HMS *Grasshopper*, where she survived the Battle of Singapore, before the ship was sunk. Judy, trapped by a falling row of lockers, was rescued by a crewman returning to look for supplies. On a deserted island she saved the surviving crew by managing to find fresh water. Then in the Dutch East Indies she trekked over 200 miles of jungle in five weeks and survived a crocodile attack. When the crew were taken POWs by the Japanese, Judy was smuggled into camp Gloegoer One, where she existed mainly on scraps of leather thrown to her by the camp's cobbler, an infantryman named Private Cousens. Judy's weight quickly dropped and her flanks began to show sharp and bony through her coat.

Meeting Leading Aircraftsman Frank Williams changed her life. He adopted her and shared his daily handful of rice with her. She would spend the rest of her days with him. In the camp Judy sometimes intervened by distracting the guards when they were administering punishment. Reciprocally, Frank Williams intervened to protect Judy from the guards, who would threaten to shoot her when she growled and barked at them.

Judy somehow managed to get pregnant and to produce more than one litter. The promise of a gift of one of her pups helped Williams convince the camp commandant – who was drunk on saké – to register her as an official POW, with the number '81A Gloegoer Medan', the only dog to be registered as a POW during World War II, thus guaranteeing her meagre food ration. From having acted as ship's mascot, Judy now provided the 1000-odd prisoners with a semblance of normality, a reminder of home, and a significant source of emotional comfort.

She moved around several more camps and survived

the sinking of the transport ship SS *Van Warwyck* during which she helped save several passengers from drowning. She was then smuggled into another camp, where she was reunited with Frank Williams. In 1945, the Japanese guards were about to put her to death following a lice outbreak among the prisoners but Williams managed to hide her until the Allied forces arrived. With the help of other prisoners, Williams smuggled Judy aboard a troop-ship and back to the UK, where she spent six months in quarantine.

After the war, Judy travelled with Williams to Tanzania, where he worked on a groundnut food scheme. She died in 1950 from a tumour, and was buried in her RAF jacket, with her various campaign medals. Frank spent two months building a granite-and-marble memorial for her, with a plaque telling her life story. Her Dickin Medal and collar were subsequently put on display at the Imperial War Museum as part of 'The Animals' War' exhibition.

Judy has further work to do here, standing in for the many other dogs famous for 'war service', such as Chips, reputedly the most decorated World War II dog, and also awarded a Dickin medal. Then there is Smoky, the Yorkshire terrier credited with twelve combat missions, awarded eight battle stars, who flew twelve air/sea rescue and photo reconnaissance missions. She survived 150 air raids on New Guinea, made it through a typhoon at Okinawa, parachuted from 30 feet out of a tree, warned her owner of incoming shells on a transport ship, and – among other tricks – could walk a tightrope while blindfolded.

L

LAIKA – FIRST DOG IN SPACE

One of the first animals in space and the first to orbit the earth was Laika, a young-ish stray mongrel from the streets of Moscow, selected for carriage within the Soviet spacecraft Sputnik 2 in November 1957. Scientists did not at that point know whether humans could survive a launch or the conditions of outer space, so flights by animals were thought a necessary precursor to human missions.

Adilya Kotovskaya, a 90-year-old Russian biologist who helped train Laika, speaking in 2017, said a bitch had been chosen because they don't have to raise a leg to urinate and so needed less space than the males. 'And [we chose] a stray because they are more resourceful and less demanding.'

While Laika may have been a trailblazer, animals had already been employed in the name of space exploration for more than a decade. The first were fruit flies blasted to an altitude of 68 miles inside a re-fashioned Nazi V2 rocket in 1947. Subsequently NASA sent several monkeys into space – including a Chimp called Ham – attached to monitoring instruments. Most died, though a monkey named Yorick (together with eleven mice) in September 1951 returned to earth alive. Soviet scientists were soon sending their own mice, rats and rabbits as one-way passengers on low-level orbits.

Laika, the first animal to actually orbit our planet and endure weightlessness, died after five hours from overheating possibly caused by technical failure – and according to some sources, panic – all alone in the tiny spacecraft and probably in severe pain. Frogs, cats and spiders have followed and in 1968 the Soviet Union sent a spacecraft to orbit the moon carrying two tortoises, wine flies and mealworms. After humans landed on the moon the following year, the contribution of animals began to diminish.

The true cause and timing of Laika's death were kept secret until 2002. The Soviet government initially claimed that she was euthanised prior to oxygen depletion or (confusingly) that she died when her oxygen ran out on day six. In 2008, Russian officials unveiled a small monument to Laika near the military research facility in Moscow that prepared her flight, portraying a dog standing on top of a rocket.

Two years later, under mounting pressure from animal rights campaigners, NASA announced that it was shelving a plan to conduct radiation experiments on squirrel monkeys. The European Space Agency also ruled out further primate tests, saying it did not see any need or use for them. As one science policy adviser has pointed out: animals, unlike human volunteers, cannot give their consent to being the subjects of experiments or to risking their lives on terrifying missions into the unknown. Nevertheless, some reports suggest that Russia may be moving ahead with plans for further primate experimentation.

LASSIE AND HER CREATOR

Lassie is the fictional dog created by Eric Knight (1897–1943), whose own story is little known. Published in 1940, Knight's bestselling novel was filmed by MGM in 1943 as *Lassie Come Home* with a rough collie named Pal playing Lassie. Pal then appeared under the same stage name in six other MGM feature films up to 1951. In addition to these sequels, the original film was followed by six television series, and was itself updated and remade in 1994 and again in 2005.

Lassie Come Home tells a simple tale. Mr and Mrs Carraclough (played by Donald Crisp and Elsa Lanchester) are hit by hard times in Yorkshire during the Depression and forced to sell their collie, Lassie, to a rich duke who has long admired her. Young Joe Carraclough (Roddy McDowall) is down-hearted at the loss of his companion. Lassie will have nothing to do with the duke and finds ways to escape her kennels and return to Joe. The duke finally takes Lassie to his home hundreds of miles away in Scotland, where his granddaughter Priscilla (Elizabeth Taylor) senses the dog's unhappiness and arranges her escape.

Lassie then sets off for the long trek back to Yorkshire, facing many dangers on the way, such as dog-catchers and a violent storm, but also meeting kind people who offer aid and comfort. At the end, Lassie – exhausted and limping – returns to her favourite resting place in the schoolyard at home where she is joyfully reunited with the boy she loves, who had given up hope of ever seeing her again.

Eric Knight, though he visited the film set, did not live to see the film: he died on 15 January 1943, aged 45, months before its release, when the transport plane on which he was travelling to Cairo crashed in the Surinam jungle. Born near Leeds, he had moved as a boy with his family to Philadelphia, where in 1917, he enlisted in Princess Patricia's Canadian light infantry, seeing action as a signaller in Flanders and France.

After that war, Knight, by now a father of three, tried unsuccessfully to establish himself as a painter and journalist. On the basis of a handful of published stories and an unimpressive first novel, he resolved to devote himself fully to writing. His first short story had been published in 1930, and for the next twelve years his fiction appeared regularly in American magazines, especially the *Saturday Evening Post* and *Esquire.* In 1940, he agreed to expand a previously published short story into a children's novel, the enduringly popular *Lassie Come Home*. With this and his final and most successful novel, *This Above All* (1941), he at last achieved literary fame and financial security.

At the end of 1942 he became an American citizen

and was promoted to the rank of major in the US army shortly before he was killed.

His only lasting monument is *Lassie Come Home*. A six-month stint in Hollywood left Knight with a distaste for the American film industry, but the movie adaptation was a big hit. According to MGM records it earned $2,613,000 in the US and Canada and $1,904,000 overseas, resulting in a profit of $2,249,000. It also launched Pal on 'the most spectacular canine career in film history'.

M

MALTESE TERRIERS AND MARY, QUEEN OF SCOTS

Mary, Queen of Scots's love of dogs, especially Maltese terriers, was a frequent source of consolation to her during her turbulent life. These small, white, long-haired and notably affectionate dogs were her companions from infancy to the scaffold. As a five-year-old child, Mary was betrothed and sent abroad to live with the French dauphin, Francis II. Uprooted, disorientated, and unable at first to speak French, she talked mainly with her Scottish governess and played with the 22 dogs at Francis's court, a collection of pugs, spaniels and Maltese terriers, which Francis used, in turn, to help teach his bride French.

When she was eighteen, Francis died, leaving Mary a widow in a foreign country. She returned to Scotland to reclaim her throne, accompanied by some favourite dogs. Scotland had become a Protestant country, and Mary was Catholic. Still, she was considered a legitimate sovereign of England by many English Catholics and, when in 1565 she married her Tudor cousin, Lord Darnley, this put further pressure on Elizabeth I – already deeply suspicious of her motives – to recognise Mary as successor to the English throne. The following year, Darnley was found dead, presumed murdered. Mary's next marriage to Lord Bothwell, believed by some to be Darnley's murderer, provoked an uprising; forced to abdicate the Scottish throne, she fled to England, seeking Elizabeth's protection – although this was not to be. Perceiving her as a threat, Elizabeth had her arrested and imprisoned for what turned out to be eighteen years. Mary was deprived of contact with friends and relatives, for fear of her plotting against the queen, and her chief companions and source of comfort were, once more, her lapdogs. Her jailor, Bess of Hardwick, reported that she spent hours talking to these dogs about her estranged son, James, and religion. Mary sent a portrait of one favourite dog to James, but it was intercepted and never reached him.

When she was charged with being an accomplice in a plot to murder Queen Elizabeth, Mary was moved to Fotheringhay Castle – damp, dark and miserable – where one comfort, again, was her lapdogs; after a direct appeal to Elizabeth she was allowed to keep them. She was brought to trial, found guilty and sentenced to death. Lord Burghley, William Cecil, had advised Elizabeth I to have Mary executed. His nephew, present at the execution on 8 February 1587, reported to Burghley that after her beheading 'her lips stirred up and down a quarter of an hour after her head was cut off', while a small dog, owned by the queen, emerged from hiding. Those present had been disturbed to see her red skirts – the colour of martyrdom – starting to move, as if her body were trying to stand. The executioner, a Mr Bull, found she had hidden her terrier puppy under her farthingale, and this dog, blood-stained and seated between her body and head, refused to leave. Eventually it was forcibly removed and washed clean. According to one report, it was then sent to France; according to another, although offered food, it refused to eat and died shortly after.

MAN AND DOG

Siegfried Sassoon appears in J.R.Ackerley's *My Dog Tulip* – both book and film – disguised as Captain Pugh, a lonely Kentish farmer, who like Ackerley himself is essentially a dog-loving loner.

Who's this – alone with stone and sky?
It's only my old dog and I –
It's only him; it's only me;
Alone with stone and grass and tree.

What share we most – we two together?
Smells, and awareness of the weather.
What is it makes us more than dust?
My trust in him; in me his trust.

Here's anyhow one decent thing
That life to man and dog can bring;
One decent thing, remultiplied
Till earth's last dog and man have died.

Siegfried Sassoon (1886–1967)

N

NANA AND J.M. BARRIE

Nana is the loyal and long-suffering dog hired on George Darling's modest income to look after his children in J.M. Barrie's *Peter Pan*. He cannot afford to employ a human nurse. Barrie specified that Nana be a black-and-white Landseer Newfoundland (like Luath, the Barries' dog at that time), though in the Disney film, Nana becomes a St Bernard. (When Barrie first conceived Peter Pan, his dog had been a St Bernard).

Darling is embarrassed to have a dog in his employ, though she is good at her job. In the original stage direction of the play, Barrie states that 'She will probably be played by a boy, if one clever enough can be found, and must never be on two legs except on those rare occasions when an ordinary nurse would be on four'. The premise of a dog-nanny is a surreal one but Barrie required a realistic execution. For the 1904 premiere, he chose an animal impersonator from a well-known theatrical family called Arthur Lupino, who wore a dog suit. In later years, when Lupino had to go to the war, he taught his wife how to take his place as the dog till he came back.

Nana is a child-loving dog, fussy, old-fashioned and

interfering, and in the last novels Barrie wrote (*Peter Pan in Kensington Gardens* (1906), *Peter and Wendy* (1911)), the family discover her in Kensington Gardens, where she irritates nursemaids out with their charges by peering into prams to look at the babies, and occasionally following them home and complaining about their care of them. Nana is described as a 'treasure', being especially thorough about bath times. She carries an umbrella in her mouth in case of rain.

Nana chases Peter Pan when he appears at the window and returns with his shadow in her mouth. She hangs it out of the window, sure that the strange boy will return for it, but Mrs Darling brings it in and rolls it up, fearing that it will look like washing and therefore 'lower the whole tone of the house'. At one point, with only a reproving glance Nana drinks some unpleasant medicine that Mr Darling maliciously pours into her bowl, telling her that he has given her a nice drink of milk. Mr Darling is cross and jealous that she has so much influence in the nursery, and he drags her outside and ties her up in the yard. Nana eventually breaks her chain, knowing that the children are in danger, and rushes to the Darling parents, who are out to dinner to warn them that they must return home. However, they are too late: the children are gone. Though Wendy likes to mother the orphaned lost boys, no adult in the play is good at parenting and thus the Darlings lose their children to Peter Pan.

Nana does not appear in the play again until the Darling children return at the end, when she displays the importance of a nurse 'who will never have another day off'. Peter Llewelyn Davies, one of the brothers who inspired the play, called *Peter Pan* 'that terrible masterpiece', before he died by suicide in 1960. Barrie himself died of pneumonia at age 77, in 1937, and jotted in a notebook: 'It is as if long after writing "P. Pan" its true meaning came to me: "desperate attempt to grow up but can't."'

NERO AND JANE WELSH CARLYLE

One morning in March 1850, Jane Welsh Carlyle's two-year-old dog Nero attempted to fly. He plummeted from the library window of their house in Cheyne Row onto the pavement below, frightening a passer-by and horrifying his owner. She took her stunned dog into her bed and indeed under her bed-clothes to hasten his recovery.

Jane was locked into an unhappy marriage with the hugely influential historian and sage Thomas Carlyle, in which the dog provided her with some of the companionship she craved. The Carlyles were childless, possibly sexless, slept in separate rooms, and both suffered from insomnia. Samuel Butler famously quipped that 'It was very good of God to let Carlyle and Mrs Carlyle marry one another, and so make only two people miserable and not four.' Though they lived together, each was increasingly alone. As one leading scholar puts this, 'Silent breakfasts, separate dinners, a shortfall of sympathy for each other's mental torment, both strangers to household joys'.

A young Greek merchant sent Nero to Jane from

Manchester in early December 1849. She was excited at the arrival of this 'perfectly beautiful and queer looking' little dog – 'Cuban (Maltese? and otherwise mongrel)' – and relieved at Thomas's amused reception of him, for Nero cunningly appeared infatuated with Carlyle. She reported to her old nurse that the 'little beast' could charm him out of his ill humour by 'danc[ing] round him on its hind legs, till he comes to and feels quite grateful for its confidence in his good-will... [and] gives it rasens [sic]... and calls it "you little villain" in a tone of great kindness'. From the start, Nero slept at the foot of Jane's bed, followed her like a shadow, lay in her lap and greatly consoled her; 'for it is really a comfort to have something alive and cheery and fond of me always there,' she wrote.

Nero neither barked nor whined, was bathed daily, got out of the yard sporadically, and was stolen more than once, always making his way back home unharmed. Standing at the open window watching the birds was one of his chief delights, and the day he attempted flight Jane wrote in a typically funny and evocative letter: 'Imagine his taking it into his head that he could fly – like the birds – if he tried! and actually trying it – out at the Library window! For a first attempt his success was not so bad; for he fairly cleared the area spikes – and tho' he did plash down on the pavement at the feet of an astonished Boy he broke no bones, was only quite stunned. He gave us a horrid fright however – was after breakfast, and – while Elizabeth was "dusting out" for Mr C. – Lying in my bed, I heard thro the deal partition Elizabeth scream; "Oh

God! Oh Nero!" and rush down stairs like a strong wind out at the street door – I sat up in my bed aghast – waiting with a feeling as of the Heavens falling till I heard her re ascending the stairs and then I sprang to meet her in my night shift. She was white as a sheet, ready to faint – could just say; "Oh take him!" the dog's body lay on her arm! "Is he killed?" I asked with terrible self-possession – "Not quite, – I think, – all BUT!" Mr C. came down from his bedroom with his chin all over soap and asked; "Has anything happened to Nero?" – "Oh Sir he must have broken all his legs, he leapt out at your window!" "God bless me!" said Mr C. and returned to finish his shaving – I sat down on the floor and laid my insensible dog over my knees, but could see no breakage – only a stun – So I took him to bed with me – under the clothes – and in an hour's time he was as brisk and active as ever. I wonder if he intends to persevere in learning to fly – for I don't think either my own or my maid's nerves can stand it.'

Nero didn't try to fly again but he had further adventures. When in 1852 Jane took a newly acquired cat – rather than Nero – onto her lap, he was very jealous. He retired under the sofa and 'neither coaxing nor cake could persuade him out; to all my blandishments he answered with an angry growl, and when I put in my hand to pull him out he retired further in, and went thro the form of snapping at it – and this mood held out for an hour or two after I had sent the cat from the room'. When he savagely attacked the interloper, Jane boxed his ears, a punishment he resented as a betrayal; after a moment's reflection, he

rushed up the stairs to the street, and left home. He was quickly found and brought back, but sulked for hours and ignored Jane.

The tussle over the cat recalls a lovers' quarrel. Indeed, later that year on 20 August Jane wrote: 'As to Nero, poor Darling… he is part and parcel of myself; when I say I am well, it means also Nero is well! Nero c'est moi! Moi c'est Nero!' Towards the end of his life, Nero figured memorably in the famous dream-like painting *A Chelsea Interior 1857–1860* by Robert Scott Tait, which shows Thomas Carlyle, Jane and Nero each inhabiting different spheres of existence, evidently estranged. Jane commented on Nero, who is caught in profile sitting on the sofa: 'Could anybody look in that dear little quadruped's face; without seeing that he was "thinking" all this nonsense of keeping him motionless on a sofa-cushion, to be painted, a great bore!'

Nero had to be put down on the last day of January 1860, when Jane was 58 and he was twelve. She recorded to Mary Russell: 'I have lost my dear little companion of eleven years' standing: my little Nero is dead! And the grief his death has caused me has been wonderful even to myself. His patience and gentleness, and loving struggle to do all his bits of duties under his painful illness, up to the last hour of his life, was very strange and touching to see, and had so endeared him to everybody in the house, that I was happily spared all reproaches for wasting so much feeling on a dog. Mr C. couldn't have reproached me, for he himself was in tears at the poor little thing's end!

And his heart was (as he phrased it) "unexpectedly and distractedly torn to pieces with it!" As for Charlotte, she went about for three days after with her face all swollen and red with weeping. But on the fourth day she got back her good looks and gay spirits; and much sooner, Mr. C. had got to speak "poor Nero", composedly enough. Only to me, whom he belonged to and whom he preferred to all living, does my dear wee dog remain a constantly recurring blank, and a thought of strange sadness!... I grieve for him as if he had been my little human child.'

When Jane was found dead in her brougham on a carriage drive in Hyde Park on 21 April 1866, her newly acquired little pug dog Tiny was on her lap. Tiny had never supplanted Nero in her affections. Carlyle testified that she 'little loved it', and 'had taken it only by charity'. He credited Nero – by contrast – for having been 'most affectionate [and] lively'. His esteem was qualified, however: he also described Nero as 'otherwise of small merit, and little or no training' and, even if 'so loyal, so loving, so naïve and true', this was 'with what of dim intellect he had!'

NIPPER

The most famous animal in the history of advertising is surely Nipper, the mixed-breed terrier on the record label who sits, head cocked, trying intently and for ever to figure out how noise is emitting from the horn of a recording device: an iconic picture of a dog trying to comprehend the human world.

Nipper, part Jack Russell, was born in Bristol in 1884. His habit of biting visitors' calves afforded his name; he was also baffled by noise from the phonograph. His first owner Mark Barraud, a Bristol painter of stage sets, who came from a family of painters of Huguenot origins, died when Nipper was only three. He was then adopted by Mark's brother Francis James Barraud, also a painter. Francis studied at the Royal Academy Schools, at Heatherley's Art School in London, and at the Beaux Arts in Antwerp: like his father Henry, he excelled at animal portraiture.

Barraud later wrote: 'It is difficult to say how the idea came to me beyond the fact that it suddenly occurred to me that to have my dog listening to the phonograph, with an intelligent and rather puzzled expression, and call it "His Master's Voice" would make an excellent subject. We had a phonograph and I often noticed how puzzled he was to make out where the voice came from. It certainly was the happiest thought I ever had.'

This account is a simplification. Nipper had been dead for three years when Barraud commemorated him in the painting, the original and cumbersome title of which was in fact *Dog Looking at and Listening to a Phonograph*. The prototype of the cylinder-driven phonograph device that so intrigues Nipper came with two needles, one for playback cylinders, the other for dictating and recording. This might explain why the dog was later described as listening to his master's voice rather than, say, Beethoven: some phonograph owners could record themselves.

This original painting was offered to and rejected by the Royal Academy and by several magazines. It was also rejected by James E. Hough of the London branch of

Edison-Bell on Charing Cross Road, who promptly and scornfully said: 'Dogs don't listen to phonographs.' On 31 May 1899, Barraud went to the Maiden Lane offices of the Gramophone Company (later morphed into EMI) with the intention of borrowing a brass horn to replace the painting's original black one. Barraud had decided to change both the colour of the horn from black to gold and the name of the painting to *His Master's Voice*. Manager William Barry Owen suggested that if the artist replaced the cylinder-based phonograph machine with one of the new Berliner disc-based gramophones, then he would buy the painting. And this accordingly happened. For the new version, Barraud was paid £50, with a further £50 for the copyright, a total roughly equivalent to £10,000 today.

Barraud went on to paint several more versions of the subject. The trademark was registered by Berliner for use in the United States on 10 July 1900, and the image became the successful emblem of the Victor and HMV record labels, HMV music stores, and the Radio Corporation of America. It was also used by Berliner Gramophone and its various affiliates, and successors, including Berliner's German subsidiary Deutsche Grammophon. Although HMV no longer exists as an imprint, having been replaced by EMI, it continues as the name of the string of retail shops.

Nipper himself died of natural causes in 1895 and was buried surrounded by magnolia trees in a small park in Clarence Street in Kingston-on-Thames. A branch of

Lloyds Bank now occupies the site. On the wall of the bank, just inside the entrance, a brass plaque commemorates the terrier that lies beneath the building. On 10 March 2010, a small road near to the dog's resting place was named Nipper Alley in his honour.

O

OGDEN NASH AND 'MAN'S BEST FRIEND'

Ogden Nash (1902–71) the American humorist is remembered for his light verse and unconventional rhymes. In 'An Introduction to Dogs', he gathers together some sharp and good-humoured observations that include his prose quip that 'A door is what a dog is perpetually on the wrong side of'. Nash champions what is facetious and what is comfortable, including the idea – first mooted by Frederick the Great – of the dog as 'man's best friend'. He ends:

> Well people may be reprehensibler
> But that's probably because they are sensibler.

OLIVER GOLDSMITH AND 'AN ELEGY ON THE DEATH OF A MAD DOG'

'An Elegy on the Death of a Mad Dog', Goldsmith's best-known poem, appeared in his novel *The Vicar of Wakefield* (1766). Its famous, startling final line – 'the dog it was that died' – is more satirical than elegiac. We are shown an apparently good and pious man who actually follows only the letter, but never the spirit, of Christianity. When Goldsmith tells us he was well liked by the townspeople he is being ironic: little is good about this man, who is really out for himself. 'The naked every day he clad,/ When he put on his clothes': he clothes himself, no one else. So, when a dog goes mad and bites this 'pious' man, the townspeople assume that he will die from the rabid bite. But in a twist, the biter, rather than the bitten, dies: 'The dog it was that died.' i.e. the man was so toxic that it's not he but the mad dog who's bitten him that ends up dead.

Good people all, of every sort,
Give ear unto my song;
And if you find it wondrous short,
It cannot hold you long.
In Islington there was a man,

Of whom the world might say
That still a godly race he ran,
Whene'er he went to pray.
A kind and gentle heart he had,
To comfort friends and foes;
The naked every day he clad,
When he put on his clothes.
And in that town a dog was found,
As many dogs there be,
Both mongrel, puppy, whelp and hound,
And curs of low degree.
This dog and man at first were friends;
But when a pique began,
The dog, to gain some private ends,
Went mad and bit the man.
Around from all the neighbouring streets
The wondering neighbours ran,
And swore the dog had lost his wits,
To bite so good a man.
The wound it seemed both sore and sad
To every Christian eye;
And while they swore the dog was mad,
They swore the man would die.
But soon a wonder came to light,
That showed the rogues they lied:
The man recovered of the bite,
The dog it was that died.

P

POLLY AND CHARLES DARWIN

In *The Descent of Man,* Charles Darwin makes use of our love of dogs as a way of convincing us that we and animals share a common ancestor. In 1871, some still found this idea shocking. In the opening chapters, he discusses whether animals possess self-consciousness or not. 'When I say to my terrier, in an eager voice…, "Hi, hi, where is it?" she at once takes it as a sign that something is to be hunted, and generally first looks quickly all around, and then rushes into the nearest thicket, to scent for any game, but, finding nothing, she looks up into any neighbouring tree for a squirrel.' He goes on to ask: 'How can we feel sure that an old dog with an excellent memory and some power of imagination, as shown by his dreams, never reflects on his past pleasures or pains in the chase?' His argument is that animals differ from humans mostly in degree, not kind, and – still using dogs as examples – he maintains that animals feel 'pleasure and pain, happiness and memory'. 'It would indeed be wonderful,' Darwin wrote, 'if, [the] mind of [an] animal was not closely allied to that of men, when the five senses were the same.'

As a youth, Darwin had been a keen fox-hunter and also loved shooting pheasant and grouse: 'I do not believe that any one could have shown more zeal for the most holy cause than I did for shooting birds,' he wrote in his autobiography. It was probably in the field that he developed his habits of keen observation. He certainly loved animals and, during their courtship, his future wife Emma was attracted by the kindness he demonstrated towards dogs and other animals. He opposed the use of traps on game reserves, and was intensely disturbed by the prospect of animals suffering for science. While maintaining that vivisection was sometimes justifiable for investigating physiology, he also called it a subject that made him 'sick with horror' and in *The Descent of Man* wrote: 'Everyone has heard of the dog suffering under vivisection, who licked the hand of the operator; this man, unless he had a heart of stone, must have felt remorse to the last hour of his life.'

During the course of his lifetime, Charles owned a dozen different dogs: a Pomeranian, a pointer, a retriever, several terriers and a Scottish deerhound. His last – and his favourite – was Polly, a sharp-witted white fox terrier 'whom' he wrote, 'I love with all my heart'. Darwin taught her to catch biscuits off her nose, and encouraged her as she barked through the window at what Darwin called 'the naughty people'. She had originally been given to his daughter Henrietta, but when Henrietta married, Darwin adopted her. Polly became his constant companion. During the hours spent in his study doing scientific research or recovering from an indisposition, Polly would often be found nearby, resting on her dog-bed. She went, too, on his daily walks around the grounds of Down House, and Darwin's son Francis recalled that his father 'was delightfully tender to Polly, and never showed any impatience at the attention she required'. Polly was both a talking point and a model for illustrations in Darwin's last book, *Expression of Emotions in Man and Animals*, in which his aim was to explore similarities not only between the anatomies of humans and animals but also between their bodily behaviour, social sympathies and facial expressions – similarities that would be additional evidence of common ancestry.

In a 1872 letter to a leading animal rights campaigner who had written an article claiming that a dog, as much as a human, was capable of love, sympathy and friendship, he wrote, 'Since publishing *The Descent of Man* I have got to believe, rather more than I did, in dogs having what may be called a conscience. When an honourable dog has committed an undiscovered offense, he certainly seems ashamed, rather than afraid to meet his master. My dog, the beloved and beautiful Polly, is, at such times, extremely affectionate to me.' The idea of a dog being honourable or dishonourable has considerable charm, especially when used as evidence of her reasoning power and moral sense. Polly died less than a month after Darwin and was buried under an apple tree near the family home.

PONGO IN *101 DALMATIANS*

As the Second World War loomed, the writer Dodie Smith sailed for New York accompanied by her husband Alec. They brought with them their pale-grey Rolls-Royce and their adored Dalmatian, Pongo. This dog had been a birthday gift from Alec in 1934 when Dodie had jestingly remarked that, since her London flat was decorated in fashionable monochrome with white carpets and black curtains, 'All I need now is a Dalmatian.' That may have been one *donné* for her best-known novel, whose hero is also called Pongo. Another was when an actress friend of Dodie's remarked 'He would make a nice fur coat.'

Dodie and Alec married in Philadelphia in 1940 and spent the next thirteen years in Hollywood, where Dodie was in demand at the film studios, and New England. The principal features of her years in the United States were journal writing and the birth of fifteen puppies in 1942 to her two Californian Dalmatians, Buzz and Folly, an event also incorporated into *The Hundred and One Dalmatians.* When the war ended, their return home was delayed in part by the prospect of quarantining their Dalmatians.

After two of her plays flopped at the Aldwych and in a spirit of defiance, Dodie Smith in 1956 wrote *The Hundred and One Dalmatians*, with its simple but compelling storyline: at a dinner party attended by a couple called Dearley, besotted owners of a pair of Dalmations, Pongo and Perdita, Cruella de Vil expresses her dislike for animals. Soon after, Pongo and Perdita have puppies, and the whole litter disappears. The Dearly dogs are now among 97 puppies kidnapped or legally purchased by Cruella's minions, with the intention of skinning them for their fur. Pongo and Perdita mount a search operation, and through the cooperation of various animals and the 'Twilight Barking', the stolen dogs are finally found in Suffolk. A rescue ensues.

The long-term survival of Dodie's novel was ensured by Disney's subsequent film adaptations: the hugely successful animated feature *101 Dalmatians* in 1961, and the 1996 live film of the same title with Glenn Close as Cruella. Dodie died on 24 November 1990, leaving an estate valued at £473,833, of which £2000 was willed to the care of Charley, her seventh and final Dalmatian.

Q

QUEENIE AND J.R. ACKERLEY

J.R. Ackerley, literary editor of the *Listener* from 1935 until 1959, wrote: 'Unable to love each other, the English turn naturally to dogs.' That was true of himself. Lonely, melancholy and unable to find a long-term gay partner, Ackerley found in his Alsatian bitch Queenie the love of his life. The story of how he acquired her from a petty criminal and gradually transferred his love from man to dog is told in his novel *We Think the World of You* (1960), made into a film with Gary Oldman and Alan Bates. It was the first of two films about Queenie. She had spent her first eighteen months scarcely exercised, tied up in a yard by her working-class owners, and thrashed when she misbehaved. She had already bitten two bus conductors and one postman and was never going to be an easy dog to care for. But for Ackerley, the relationship with her satisfied some profound psychological need and also inspired his passionate advocacy of animal rights.

Four years earlier, in 1956, Ackerley had published *My Dog Tulip*, a shockingly frank and funny portrait of Queenie ('Tulip' in the book), arguably one of the most important books about a dog ever published. As a vet points out: Queenie was in love with Ackerley and spent energy protecting him from other people. She was passionately jealous and possessive. Ackerley wryly notes that his friends, in turn, 'seemed to resent being challenged whenever they approach[ed] their own sitting or dining rooms'. They stopped visiting and also stopped inviting him.

Rosamund Lehmann called this the only 'dog book' to record human–animal love in terms of absolute equality. Indeed, although Ackerley loved Queenie deeply, he never expects us to do the same. Chapter 2, entitled 'Liquids and Solids' and concerned with urination and excretion, still has the power to embarrass or disgust, or both. Ackerley, sometimes thought a misanthropist, had no difficulty with this. 'I think that people ought to be upset,' he wrote; 'I think that life is so important and, in its workings, so upsetting that nobody should be spared.'

He notes how the scent or secretion of the anal glands, which is what dogs sniff, is one complex source of social information, a language, a code. Urine is another. Thus Queenie loves to sprinkle onto bones, fish, bread, vomit, socks, and any other item of interest excepting food she wishes to eat. Ackerley is curious to see how Queenie might behave towards a human corpse recovered from the Thames, and fends off readerly censoriousness with the criticism that 'human beings are so arrogant', taking a side-swipe at human cruelty in – and here Ackerley takes a bizarre example – decapitating pigs then disfiguring their heads. He is on a crusade to tell the truth.

When Tulip elects to urinate to cover Ackerley's pee, he comments, with a comical humility: 'How touched I was! How honoured I felt! Oh Tulip! Thank you… I feel a proper dog.'

Tulip/Queenie has a propensity towards multiple bowel movements – three or four per walk – and is not particular about where she relieves herself. When a passing cyclist criticises Ackerley (who has no garden) for allowing her to soil the pavement, he responds with scatological name-calling: 'Turds like you… arseholes.' When she shits in front of a greengrocers he, after some prevarication, agrees to clean up, but starts another row by requesting that the shopkeeper thank him publicly.

One key episode involves an invitation to stay with a Captain Pugh in Kent, a solitary figure based on Ackerley's friend, the poet Siegfried Sassoon. Ackerley is 'deeply touched' when Queenie kisses his cheek before showing how carefully she has chosen a spot to excrete her very loose stools, against Captain Pugh's door. 'How wonderful to have an animal communicate… to ask a personal favour…' He spends 20 minutes swabbing up the mess, using the paper lining from a chest of drawers. Ackerley and Tulip are not asked again.

Ackerley's book is packed with interesting and accurate observation and he creates a comical double perspective, both human and canine. When Queenie needs to make herself sick, she eats coarse grass; when she is on heat, he offers hand pressure on her vulva: 'just a little finger-work' he is said to have remarked, cryptically, to Olivia

Manning. His comical attempts to mate her occupy some space, as does his uncertainty about what to do with her litter, once mating is successful: he contemplates drowning the female pups but mercifully desists.

Nobody writes better than Ackerley about the moving interdependence of man and dog, about the sheer life-and-death power owners have over their pets. His book was made into an excellent digitally animated film in 2009, which ends with Ackerley's wise and moving words:

> What strained and anxious lives dogs must lead, so emotionally involved in the world of humans, whose affections they strive endlessly to secure, whose authority they are expected unquestioningly to obey, and whose mind they can never do more than imperfectly reach and comprehend. Stupidly loved, stupidly hated, acquired without thought, reared and ruled without understanding, passed on or 'put to sleep' without care, did they, I wondered, these descendants of the creature who, thousands of years ago in the primeval forests, laid siege to the heart of man, took him under their protection, tried to tame him, and failed... did they suffer from headaches?

Queenie died in 1961, at the age of sixteen.

R

RECIPES FOR COOKING AND EATING DOG

During the Cultural Revolution, keeping a cat or dog in China was so dangerous that pets were sometimes hidden away in urban flats for years in case a neighbour reported you and you were violently punished for 'bourgeois behaviour'. Many thought the joys of living with a pet worth this risk. The love of dogs is deep in China. So, however, is the eating of dogs (as also in Korea and Vietnam). There are some horrifying and deeply upsetting YouTube videos that can tell you more than you may wish to know about this. (Dog-eating was one of the main reasons Iris Murdoch gave for finding visiting China unnerving). That starving Parisians ate their own dogs and cats during the Siege of 1870 still has the power to shock.

ROMULUS AND REMUS

The legend that Romulus and Remus, founders of Rome, were suckled by a she-wolf, has always seemed fabulous. A strange echo, however, was recorded (for a programme on Radio 4) on a Norfolk farm in the harsh winter of 1947. The farmer's wife, who was interviewed for the programme, noticed that her milk was drying up and she had no supply of food that might replenish her. As a result, her baby was literally starving. Her Alsatian bitch, on the other hand, who had also just littered, did have a supply of dog food. In desperation the farmer's wife wondered whether the dog might allow a human baby to suckle together with her pups. She carefully shaved and disinfected the dog's nipples and the dog readily accepted her human foster-child for the weeks it took for the weather to break. The story ended happily, and the child always referred humorously to the pups as his half-siblings.

RUDYARD KIPLING AND 'THE POWER OF THE DOG'

Kipling (1865–1936) loved dogs and enjoyed a close bond with them throughout his life. As his biographer Andrew Lycett observes, Kipling's dogs often took on the role of close companion or consort. In his 1899 story 'Garm – a Hostage', Kipling describes how the narrator's dog, Vixen, slept in his bed with him at night. A dog also features in another early tale, 'The Dog Hervey' (1914). Kipling later came up with the innovative idea – before Virginia Woolf's *Flush* – of writing a story from a dog's perspective. 'Thy Servant, a Dog' (1930) is narrated with a simplified vocabulary in a strange patois by an Aberdeen terrier named Boots. An example:

> There is walk-in-park-on-lead. There is off-lead-when-we-come-to-the-grass. There is 'nother dog, like me, off-lead. I say: 'Name?' He says: 'Slippers.' He says: 'Name?' I say: 'Boots.' He says: 'I am fine dog. I have Own God called Miss.' I say: 'I am very-fine dog. I have Own God called Master.' There is walk-round-on-toes.

This facetiousness can tire after a while. But no one writes better than Kipling about how dog-ownership guarantees that your heart will be broken if – as is likely – your dog dies before you do, as he does here in 'The Power of the Dog' (1922):

> There is sorrow enough in the natural way
> From men and women to fill our day;
> And when we are certain of sorrow in store,
> Why do we always arrange for more?
> *Brothers and sisters, I bid you beware*
> *Of giving your heart to a dog to tear.*
>
> Buy a pup and your money will buy
> Love unflinching that cannot lie –
> Perfect passion and worship fed
> By a kick in the ribs or a pat on the head.
> *Nevertheless it is hardly fair*
> *To risk your heart for a dog to tear.*
>
> When the fourteen years which Nature permits
> Are closing in asthma, or tumour, or fits,
> And the vet's unspoken prescription runs
> To lethal chambers or loaded guns,
> *Then you will find – it's your own affair –*
> *But... you've given your heart to a dog to tear.*
>
> When the body that lived at your single will,
> With its whimper of welcome, is stilled (how still!),

When the spirit that answered your every mood
Is gone – wherever it goes – for good,
You will discover how much you care,
And will give your heart to a dog to tear!

We've sorrow enough in the natural way,
When it comes to burying Christian clay.
Our loves are not given, but only lent,
At compound interest of cent per cent,
Though it is not always the case, I believe,
That the longer we've kept 'em, the more do we grieve;
For, when debts are payable, right or wrong,
A short-time loan is as bad as a long –
So why in – Heaven (before we are there)
Should we give our hearts to a dog to tear?

S

SHAKESPEARE'S DISLIKE OF DOGS

Shakespeare is often hailed as the most invisible of writers; nothing about his private life can be gleaned from his work, except – perhaps – for one very un-English peccadillo: he disliked dogs. The eminent Shakespeare scholar Professor Stephen Greenblatt was involved in a lively correspondence on this matter in the *New York Review of Books* in 2009. For horses, rabbits, even snails, Greenblatt argues, Shakespeare felt a deep, inward understanding, but with dogs his imagination curdled. This much had already been noticed in 1935 in Caroline Spurgeon's landmark study of Shakespeare's imagery: dogs function in his work almost entirely negatively. He routinely associated man's best friend with fawning flatterers, greedily licking up whatever treats anyone offers them, or with snarling, 'venom-mouthed' ingrates.

It is true that *A Midsummer Night's Dream* (IV. i) contains the magnificently lyrical exchange:

HIPPOLYTA:
I was with Hercules and Cadmus once
When in a wood of Crete they bayed the bear

With hounds of Sparta. Never did I hear
Such gallant chiding; for, besides the groves,
The skies, the fountains, every region near
Seemed all one mutual cry. I never heard
So musical a discord, such sweet thunder.

THESEUS:
My hounds are bred out of the Spartan kind,
So flewed, so sanded; and their heads are hung
With ears that sweep away the morning dew,
Crook-kneed, and dew-lapped like Thessalian bulls,
Slow in pursuit, but matched in mouth like bells,
Each under each. A cry more tuneable
Was never holla'd to nor cheer'd with horn
In Crete, in Sparta, nor in Thessaly.
Judge when you hear.

Regarding this passage, the Victorian political commentator Walter Bagehot remarked that Shakespeare must have been both a judge of dogs and an out-of-doors sporting man. A passage from the Induction to *The Taming of the Shrew* starting 'Huntsman, I charge thee, tender well my hounds… I would not lose the dog for twenty pound' might lead to the same conclusion. Greenblatt, however, demurs. Shakespeare is merely mimicking the way aristocrats prized their skilled hunting dogs, valuing them more highly than they did the poor peasants who worked their fields.

Moreover, many passages use dog as shorthand for

something base. In *Julius Caesar* (III. i) Mark Antony predicts the anarchy and cruelty of civil strife using dogs to depict the breakdown of civilised behaviour:

> … All pity choked with custom of fell deeds;
> And Caesar's spirit, ranging for revenge,
> With Ate by his side come hot from hell,
> Shall in these confines with a monarch's voice
> Cry Havoc and let slip the dogs of war,
> That this foul deed shall smell above the earth
> With carrion men groaning for burial.

Shakespeare's dog insults are legion: 'whoreson dog' (*Cymbeline, King Lear,* and *Troilus* and *Cressida*); 'slave, soulless villain, dog' (*Antony and Cleopatra*); 'egregious dog? O viper vile!' (*Henry V*); 'cut throat dog' (*The Merchant of Venice*). When Richard III is killed, victorious Richmond proclaims: 'The day is ours, the bloody dog is dead.' In *Coriolanus*, the rabble may be turned against Coriolanus 'as easy/As to set dogs on sheep'. The same image is used in *Richard III*. Dogs can be cowards; they bark and bay, fight and steal. When authority appears hollow, King Lear laments that even 'a dog's obeyed in office'. In the same play, the villainous sisters Goneril and Regan are 'dog-hearted' – a quality shared with the 'hell-hound' Richard of Gloucester and with the fathomlessly malevolent Iago ('O damned Iago! O inhuman dog').

When Shakespeare's dogs are not snarling and biting, they are servile flatterers, recalling craven courtiers:

'Why, what a candy deal of courtesy,' Hotspur remarks of Bolingbroke, 'this fawning greyhound then did proffer me!' (*Henry IV Part One*, I. iii). Such displays of canine flattery must never be trusted: 'When he fawns, he bites; and when he bites,/His venom tooth will rankle to the death' (*Richard III* I. iii). And when they try to make friends, dogs are just toadying to us. King Lear complains of his vengeful daughters, 'They flatter'd me like a dog.'

That dogs flatter and fawn is a theme in the Comedies just as much as in the Histories and Tragedies. Helena in *A Midsummer Nights Dream* (II. i) refers to the servility of dogs:

> And even for that do I love you the more.
> I am your spaniel. And, Demetrius,
> The more you beat me, I will fawn on you.
> Use me but as your spaniel – spurn me, strike me,
> Neglect me, lose me. Only give me leave,
> Unworthy as I am, to follow you.
> What worser place can I beg in your love
> – And yet a place of high respect with me –
> Than to be usèd as you use your dog?

Only one dog actually appears on stage in Shakespeare (if we except the nameless animal presented in the play-within-the-play in *A Midsummer Nights Dream*): Crab in *The Two Gentlemen of Verona*. His owner, the clown Lance, observes that dogs lack all feeling. When Lance has to leave the household, everyone is touched by his departure – 'My mother weeping, my father wailing, my sister crying, our maid howling, our cat wringing her hands' – except for their dog Crab: 'He is a stone, a very pebble-stone, and has no more pity in him than a dog' (II. iii). Even a Jew, Lance remarks, would have wept at the parting, but Crab did not shed a tear.

Lance often appears before the audience delivering silly monologues about his relationship with his beloved Crab. When Crab gets caught pissing under the duke's table, rather than allow Crab to be whipped Lance takes both the blame and the punishment for supposedly wetting his pants:

> all the chamber smelt him. 'Out
> with the dog!' says one: 'What cur is that?' says
> another. 'Whip him out!' says the third. 'Hang him
> up!' says the duke. I, having been acquainted with
> the smell before, knew it was Crab, and goes me to
> the fellow that whips the dogs. 'Friend,' quoth I,
> 'you mean to whip the dog?' 'Ay, marry, do I,'
> quoth he. 'You do him the more wrong,' quoth I;
> ''Twas I did the thing you wot of.' He makes me no
> more ado but whips me out of the chamber. How
> many masters would do this for his servant?...
> Did not I bid thee still mark me, and do as I do?
> When didst thou see me heave up my leg and make
> water against a gentlewoman's farthingale? Didst
> thou ever see me do such a trick? (IV. iv)

Lance has endured other punishments for Crab's misbehaviour. He stood in the stocks when Crab stole some 'puddings' and in a pillory when Crab killed a neighbour's geese (IV. iv). Lance's excessive devotion to Crab may parody the human love plots; but it also stands as one of the few occasions when Shakespeare acknowledges that dogs, albeit irrationally, earn our affection.

SHEEPDOG TRIALS IN HYDE PARK

A shepherd stands at one end of the arena.
Five sheep are unpenned at the other. His dog runs out
In a curve to behind them, fetches them straight to the
shepherd,
Then drives the flock round a triangular course
Through a couple of gates and back to his master: two
Must be sorted there from the flock, then all five penned.
Gathering, driving away, shedding and penning
Are the plain words for the miraculous game.

An abstract game. What can the sheepdog make of such
Simplified terrain? – no hills, dales, bogs, walls, tracks,
Only a quarter-mile plain of grass, dumb crowds
Like crowds on hoardings around it, and behind them
Traffic or mounds of lovers and children playing.
Well, the dog is no landscape-fancier: his whole concern
Is with his master's whistle, and of course
With the flock – sheep are sheep anywhere for him.

The sheep are the chanciest element. Why, for instance,
Go through this gate when there's on either side of it

No wall or hedge but huge and viable space?
Why not eat the grass instead of being pushed around it?
Like a blob of quicksilver on a tilting board
The flock erratically runs, dithers, breaks up,
Is reassembled: their ruling idea is the dog;
And behind the dog, though they know it not yet, is
  a shepherd.

The shepherd knows that time is of the essence
But haste calamitous. Between dog and sheep
There is always an ideal distance, a perfect angle;
But these are constantly varying, so the man
Should anticipate each move through the dog,
  his medium.
The shepherd is the brain behind the dog's brain,
But his control of dog, like dog's of sheep,
Is never absolute – that's the beauty of it.

For beautiful it is. The guided missiles,
The black-and-white angels follow each quirk and jink of

The evasive sheep, play grandmother's-steps
  behind them,
Freeze to the ground, or leap to head off a straggler
Almost before it knows that it wants to stray,
As if radar-controlled. But they are not machines –
You can feel them feeling mastery, doubt, chagrin:
Machines don't frolic when their job is done.

What's needfully done in the solitude of sheep-runs –
Those rough, real tasks become this stylised game,
A demonstration of intuitive wit
Kept natural by the saving grace of error.
To lift, to fetch, to drive, to shed, to pen
Are acts I recognise, with all they mean
Of shepherding the unruly, for a kind of
Controlled woolgathering is my work too.

Cecil Day-Lewis (1904–72)

SIR WALTER RALEIGH AND 'AN UNRULY AND ILL-MANNERED DOG'

'To A Lady With An Unruly And Ill-Mannered Dog Who Bit Several Persons Of Importance' is a long title for a short and slight poem. Its author, Sir Walter Raleigh (1861–1922), was not the Elizabethan explorer/poet but the first person to hold a Chair in English Literature at the University of Oxford. Before that he was Regius Professor at Glasgow. The poem is free of sentimentality, presenting a dog's aggression as a timely and refreshing memento mori. The threat of being bitten by a dog and possibly contracting a serious disease, such as rabies (see Stanza 2's reference to a 'hydrophobic end') keeps humans on their toes, since it reminds us of our own mortality and helps put ordinary day-to-day worries – 'careless cooks, and warts, and debt' – into perspective.

Your dog is not a dog of grace;
He does not wag the tail or beg;
He bit Miss Dickson in the face;
He bit a Bailie in the leg.

What tragic choices such a dog
Presents to visitor or friend!
Outside there is the Glasgow fog;
Within, a hydrophobic end.

Yet some relief even terror brings,
For when our life is cold and gray
We waste our strength on little things,
And fret our puny souls away.

A snarl! A scruffle round the room!
A sense that Death is drawing near!
And human creatures reassume
The elemental robe of fear.

So when my colleague makes his moan
Of careless cooks, and warts, and debt,
– Enlarge his views, restore his tone,
And introduce him to your Pet!

Quod Raleigh.

SNOWY AND TINTIN

The Adventures of Tintin by Belgian cartoonist Georges Remi (1907–83), who wrote under the pen name Hergé, was one of the most popular comics of all time, published in more than 70 languages with sales of more than 200 million copies and many adaptations, including an animated film by Stephen Spielberg. Its hero Tintin is a courageous young Belgian reporter who rarely files a story but has exciting adventures instead, aided by his faithful dog Snowy, a white wire fox terrier who acts as side-kick and companion, sniffing, tracking, chasing and biting.

Snowy is fearless against much larger creatures when Tintin is threatened. He repeatedly frees Tintin from captivity, saves him from danger, and will sometimes identify a villain before him. Snowy also butts into everyone's business, noses out important clues and provides comic relief. Throughout the first eight stories, Snowy is the series' co-star, able to understand human language, communicating via speech bubbles with internal monologues, jokes, warnings and pleas to Tintin to exercise caution. He takes an interest in mechanics and geography and can quote the Bible.

Snowy has three weaknesses: a fondness for Scotch whisky, leading to bouts of drinking that get him into trouble, a fear of spiders and a passion for chewing bones that creates moral dilemmas when he has to decide between carrying out an important task, such as relaying an SOS message, and indulging in his bone-gnawing habit. But Snowy is irrepressibly loyal to Tintin and always wishes to stay by his master's side: in a scene in *The Shooting Star* when Tintin temporarily abandons him, Snowy is inconsolable.

Hergé never had a dog until his last years; however, in 1929, he was a regular at a café where the proprietor had a terrier that helped inspire Snowy. The dog's original French name Milou was the nickname of Hergé's first girlfriend. Snowy debuted on 10 January 1929 in the first instalment of *Tintin in the Land of the Soviets* and his character evolved over time.

In early works, he converses with other characters including animals, and provides a dry and cynical side-commentary on each situation, balancing Tintin's constantly upbeat optimism. After the introduction of Captain Haddock in the ninth story, *The Crab with the Golden Claws*, Snowy's speaking role diminishes and the captain takes over the role of cynic, Snowy gradually shifting into a more light-hearted role, talking only with Tintin.

SPOILED DOGS

You can be soft-hearted with your dogs and spoil them and yet be callous in relation to your fellow human beings. A case in hand might be that of Chaucer's Prioress, a woman of contradictions, who, though a person of faith, has the affectation of trying to speak French like a lady of the court.

She is described in the Prologue of *The Canterbury Tales* as follows:

> As for her sympathies and tender feelings,
> She was so charitably solicitous
> She used to weep if she but saw a mouse
> Caught in a trap, if it were dead or bleeding,
> And she had little dogs she would be feeding
> With roasted flesh, or milk, or fine white bread.
> And bitterly she wept if one were dead
> Or someone took a stick and made it smart;
> She was all sentiment and tender heart.

For all her tender heart, the Prioress prefers dogs to people, and the tale she tells concerns the Jews' murder of a Christian child before throwing his body on a dung heap. The Jews are then drawn apart by horses before being hanged.

T

THOMAS HARDY'S WESSEX

Wessex aka Wessie was Thomas Hardy's beloved dog of thirteen years – a combative fox terrier who loved listening to the radio and whom Lady Cynthia Asquith described as 'the most despotic dog guests have ever suffered under'. J.M. Barrie was not alone in claiming Wessex was allowed to walk about unchecked on the dinner table, contesting every forkful he wished to eat. The dog also shredded the trouser legs of several guests and nipped both the postman and Hardy's fellow writer John Galsworthy. Hardy wrote two poems about Wessex after his death in 1926, 'Dead Wessex' and 'A Popular Personage at Home', of which the latter is by far the stronger, written successfully from the dog's perspective. Still, he ends up sounding like his owner, pondering the transience of life.

A Popular Personage at Home:

'I live here: "Wessex" is my name:
I am a dog known rather well:
I guard the house but how that came

To be my whim I cannot tell.

'With a leap and a heart elate I go
At the end of an hour's expectancy
To take a walk of a mile or so
With the folk I let live here with me.

'Along the path, amid the grass
I sniff, and find out rarest smells
For rolling over as I pass
The open fields toward the dells.

'No doubt I shall always cross this sill,
And turn the corner, and stand steady,
Gazing back for my Mistress till
She reaches where I have run already,

'And that this meadow with its brook,
And bulrush, even as it appears
As I plunge by with hasty look,
Will stay the same a thousand years.'

Thus 'Wessex.' But a dubious ray
At times informs his steadfast eye,
Just for a trice, as though to say,
'Yet, will this pass, and pass shall I?'

THE *TITANIC* AND ITS DOGS

The *Titanic* disaster portended a tragic century. The ship was advertised as the biggest, safest and fastest ever made, designed to reach New York in record time. Four days after she left Southampton on her maiden voyage on 10 April 1912, she struck an iceberg in fog and darkness, tearing five hull compartments open. A swift and horrifying nemesis followed. The *Titanic* had only half the requisite life-boats and, out of a total of around 2229 people, 1517 drowned. The first lifeboat, although it could carry 65 people, left with only 28 on board. Between 701 and 713 in all survived.

The *Titanic* was dog-friendly. About twelve dogs owned by passengers were kept in the excellent kennel facilities on F Deck, and it was the job of the ship's carpenter John Hutchison to take care of them. He, a steward or one of the bellboys provided the dogs with bathroom breaks and daily exercise on deck. These walks were much looked forward to, as a time when the dogs could be admired and petted by all. A dog show was even mooted for 15 April but the ship had already sunk by then.

John Jacob Astor, the richest person aboard – indeed

one of the richest men in the world – who himself perished, brought his beloved Airedale, Kitty, with him.

Other passengers who died with their dogs on the *Titanic* included horse-breeder William Dulles and his fox terrier and 50-year-old Ann Isham, who was thought unusual because she used to visit her Great Dane in her kennel on Deck F. Few other dog-owners bothered. When the lifeboats were lowered, the Great Dane was clearly too large for them but Anne refused to leave her dog behind and insisted that she would do what was needed to save him. An often repeated story tells how, after the sinking, a body that might have been hers was observed in the water with its arms frozen around a dog. She was one of only four women travelling first class who died in the disaster.

Harry Anderson, who survived, brought a chow, for whose loss he claimed $50. Robert Daniel, an American banker, who also survived, was offered $750 in compensation for the loss of his dog, a champion French bulldog with the impressive name Gamin de Pycombe whom he had bought in England for the extraordinary price of £150 (£14,000 in today's money). William Carter, another survivor, lost his elderly Airedale and another dog – a King Charles spaniel or a Pekinese.

A number of lapdogs were secreted within first-class cabins and state rooms, the crew perhaps tipped to turn a blind eye. The American painter Francis David Miller – last seen helping women and children into lifeboats before he drowned – wrote disapprovingly in a letter sent from the *Titanic's* last stop, Queenstown in Ireland: 'Looking over the [passenger] list I only find three or four people I know but there are... a number of obnoxious, ostentatious American women, the scourge of any place they infest, and worse on shipboard than anywhere. Many of them carry tiny dogs, and lead husbands around like pet lambs.'

Helen Bishop claimed that the reason Frou Frou, her toy dog of unknown breed, was allowed to stay in her cabin was because the stewards considered it 'too pretty' to put among the bigger dogs in the kennels. Helen, who was nineteen and pregnant, survived together with her newly-wed husband. Later, she would tell tearfully how, as she left her state room for the last time, Frou Frou grabbed the hem of her dress, trying to keep her from going. She felt obliged to leave her dog behind and was remembered as one of those who helped row her lifeboat to safety.

Like all ships, the *Titanic* had a rat population and on the eve of the sinking one shocked the third-class diners by running across the dining room: some women burst into tears, while men tried (unsuccessfully) to capture it. The ship also had her own official cat, Jenny, kept as a mascot and encouraged to keep down the rodent population. Transferred from the *Titanic's* sister ship *Olympic*, Jenny gave birth in the week before the doomed liner sailed from Southampton. She lived in the galley, where the victualling staff fed her and her kittens on scraps. Stewardess Violet Jessop wrote that the cat 'laid her family near Jim, the scullion, whose approval she always sought and who always gave her warm devotion'.

There were also birds aboard. Ella Holmes White of New York brought four roosters and hens from France, intending to improve her poultry stock at home. Another woman was said to have boarded 30 cockerels. Elizabeth Ramel Nye brought her yellow canary (they left at Cherbourg). Each animal travelled on its own ticket. The canary's ticket cost 25 US cents.

When disaster struck, an unknown passenger went to the kennels to release all the dogs in an attempt to spare them the horror of drowning in locked cages. These dogs then raced hectically up and down the slanting, sinking deck. None survived.

This did not stop an apocryphal story appearing in the *New York Herald* one day after *Titanic* survivors on the *Carpathia* docked in New York on 18 April. The legend runs as follows: the Scots first officer, William McMaster Murdoch, who died, had with him a large, black Newfoundland dog named Rigel. While other dogs die in cold water, Newfoundlands are supposedly bred to function in harsh North Atlantic conditions, their webbed feet, rudder-like tail and water-resistant coat plus the same mechanisms to combat hypothermia that polar bears possess allowing these dogs to help retrieve fishing nets off the shores of their home island, 400 miles north of where the *Titanic* sank. There are indeed authenticated stories of Newfoundlands rescuing people from the icy sea.

Rigel swam around, at first apparently desperately

looking for his master, but after a while choosing simply to stay close to Lifeboat 4. The dog was too large to bring on board even had there been space to do so, but the humans, in their exposed lifeboat, suffered more from the effects of the wet and cold than Rigel did from the freezing water. Some hours after the *Titanic* went down, the passenger ship *Carpathia* arrived and began to pick up surviving passengers.

It was still dark and a low mist hung on the water. *Carpathia's* crew was calling out and waiting for lifeboat passengers to respond in order to locate them. Lifeboat 4 was separated from the other lifeboats by some distance. Finally, the *Carpathia* began to pull away from the area, unknowingly on a course directly bearing down on the unseen little lifeboat. Its passengers were simply too weak to shout loudly enough to avoid being run down by the ship. But Rigel was still strong enough to bark. *Carpathia's* Captain, Arthur Henry Rostron, heard the dog and ordered the ship to stop. Swimming in front of the lifeboat, the dog marked the location of the survivors, all of whom were hauled up the starboard gangway.

This story reappeared in a well-known book, *The Sinking of the Titanic and Great Sea Disasters*, first published in 1912 only months after the shipwreck. Alas, few if any of the details of this story have been verified. Almost certainly it was invented by a crewman for gain at a moment when newspapers were hungry for picturesque tales and willing to pay good money for them.

TO A BLACK GREYHOUND

Shining black in the shining light,
Inky black in the golden sun,
Graceful as the swallow's flight,
Light as swallow, winged one,
Swift as driven hurricane –
Double-sinewed stretch and spring,
Muffled thud of flying feet,
See the black dog galloping,
Hear his wild foot-beat.

See him lie when the day is dead,
Black curves curled on the boarded floor.
Sleepy eyes, my sleepy-head –
Eyes that were aflame before.
Gentle now, they burn no more;
Gentle now and softly warm,
With the fire that made them bright
Hidden – as when after storm
Softly falls the night.

God of speed, who makes the fire –
God of Peace, who lulls the same –
God who gives the fierce desire,
Lust for blood as fierce as flame –
God who stands in Pity's name –
Many may ye be or less,
Ye who rule the earth and sun:
Gods of strength and gentleness,
Ye are ever one.

Julian Grenfell (1888–1915)

TODDY, WHISKY AND KARL MARX

Karl Marx thought dogs organised their own society better than capitalists did: cooperatively, rather than exploitatively. In 1877, Marx, who lived in London, joined the Dogberry Club, founded by his daughter Eleanor together with some friends, for fortnightly play-reading and other thespian activities relating to Shakespeare. Marx loved Shakespeare and having fun with friends, often laughing until the tears ran down his face.

He also loved dogs. In 1922, a fellow member of the club, Marian Comyn recorded her memories of him, which include this charming vignette:

> Karl Marx was fond of dogs, and three small animals of no particular breed – of a mixture of many breeds indeed – formed important members of the household. One was called Toddy, another Whisky – the name of the third I forget, but I fancy that, too, was alcoholic. They were all three sociable little beasts, ever ready for a romp, and very affectionate. One day, after an absence of six weeks in Scotland, I went to see Eleanor and found her with her father in the

drawing-room, playing with Whisky. Whisky at once transferred his attentions to me, greeting me with ebullient friendliness, but almost immediately he ran to the door and whined to have it opened for him. Eleanor said: 'He has gone down to Toddy, who has just presented him with some puppies.'

She had hardly finished speaking before there was a scratching and scrambling in the hall, and in bounded Whisky, shepherding Toddy. The little mother made straight for me, exchanged affabilities in friendly fashion, then hurried back to her family. Whisky meanwhile stood on the rug, wagging a proudly contented tail, and looking from one to the other, as who should say: 'See how well I know how to do the right thing.'

Dr. Marx was much impressed by this exhibition of canine intelligence. He observed that it was clear the dog had gone downstairs to tell his little mate an old friend had arrived, and it was her bounden duty to come and pay her respects without delay. Toddy, like an exemplary wife, had torn herself away from her squealing babies, in order to do his bidding.

TOLSTOI'S DOGS

In Part 6 of Tolstoi's *Anna Karenina*, a spot-and-tan pointer called Krak puts his paws up onto his master Oblonsky's chest, to express affection and excitement. He is closely observed by Laska, the setter belonging to Levin. These hunting dogs are in competition for game, like their owners. We learn in a later chapter that Laska also longs to put her paws up onto Levin's chest but lacks the courage to do so.

It is a symptom of Tolstoi's god-like empathy that he dares to show us the world through a dog's consciousness. In *War and Peace*, the simple but wise and contented peasant Platon Karataev has life-affirming understanding and a touching, natural affinity for his dog Sashenka. Tolstoi's dogs are sometimes smarter than their owners but they know – just as do his wise peasants – that they must remember to appear subordinate. The dogs in *Anna Karenina* are frustrated and confused when they spot and point out quarry to the humans who, instead of pursuing the birds and firing, ignore them. Thus Laska is awarded autonomy. Twice, when given incomprehensible commands, she 'pretends' to obey in order to make Levin feel better.

Laska stopped, looked ironically at the horses and inquiringly at Levin. Levin patted Laska, and whistled as a sign that she might begin. Laska ran joyfully and anxiously through the slush that swayed under her… Running into the marsh among the familiar scents of roots, marsh plants, and slime and the extraneous smell of horse dung, Laska detected at once a smell that pervaded the whole marsh, the scent of that strong-smelling bird that always excited her more than any other. Here and there among the moss and marsh plants this scent was very strong, but it was impossible to determine in which direction it grew stronger or fainter. To find the direction, she had to go further away from the wind. Not feeling the motion of her legs, Laska bounded with a stiff gallop, so that at each bound she could stop short, to the right, away from the wind that blew from the east before sunrise, and turned facing the wind. Sniffing in the air with dilated nostrils, she felt at once that not their tracks only but they themselves were here before her, and not one, but many. Laska slackened her speed. They were here, but where precisely she could not yet determine.

To find the very spot, she began to make a circle, when suddenly her master's voice drew her off. 'Laska! here?' he asked, pointing her to a different direction. She stopped, asking him if she had better not go on doing as she had begun. But he repeated his command in an angry voice, pointing to a spot covered with water, where there could not be anything. She obeyed him, pretending she was looking, so as to please him, went round it, and went back to her former position, and was at once aware of the scent again. Now when he was not hindering her, she knew what to do, and without looking at what was under her feet, and to her vexation stumbling over a high stump into the water, but righting herself with her strong, supple legs, she began making the circle which was to make all clear to her. The scent of them reached her, stronger and stronger, and more and more defined, and all at once it became perfectly clear to her that one of them was here, behind this tuft of reeds, five paces in front of her; she stopped, and her whole body was still and rigid. On her short legs she could see nothing in front of her, but by the scent she knew it was sitting not more than five paces off. She stood still, feeling more and more conscious of it, and enjoying it in anticipation. Her tail was stretched straight and tense, and only wagging at the extreme end. Her mouth was slightly open, her ears raised. One ear had been turned wrong side out as she ran up, and she breathed heavily but warily, and still more warily looked round, but more with her eyes than her head, to her master. He was coming along with the face she knew so well, though the eyes were always terrible to her. He stumbled over the stump as he came, and moved, as she thought, extraordinarily slowly. She thought he came slowly, but he was running.

Noticing Laska's special attitude as she crouched on the ground, as it were scratching big prints with her hind paws, and with her mouth slightly open, Levin knew she was pointing at grouse, and with an inward prayer for luck, especially with the first bird, he ran up to her. Coming quite close up to her, he could from his height look beyond her, and he saw with his eyes what she was seeing with her nose. In a space between two little thickets, at a couple of yards' distance, he could see a grouse. Turning its head, it was listening. Then lightly preening and folding its wings, it disappeared round a corner with a clumsy wag of its tail.

'Fetch it, fetch it!' shouted Levin, giving Laska a shove from behind.

'But I can't go,' thought Laska. 'Where am I to go? From here I feel them, but if I move forward I shall know nothing of where they are or who they are.'

But then he shoved her with his knee, and in an excited whisper said, 'Fetch it, Laska.'

'Well, if that's what he wishes, I'll do it, but I can't answer for myself now,' she thought, and darted forward as fast as her legs would carry her between the thick bushes. She scented nothing now; she could only see and hear, without understanding anything.'

TOTO IN *THE WIZARD OF OZ*

Toto lives with Dorothy on her aunt and uncle's Kansas farm where he plays a leading role. When he bites their strict neighbour Miss Almira Gulch on the leg, she obtains a sheriff's order for him to be put down. He escapes and returns to Dorothy, who decides to run away, but just then a tornado strikes and the house is sent spinning in the air, landing in Munchkinland in the Land of Oz.

As Dorothy, Toto and companions make their way to the Witch's castle, the Witch captures them and plots to kill Dorothy in order to steal her slippers. It is Toto who pulls back the curtain in the castle to expose the 'Wizard' as a middle-aged man operating machinery and speaking into a microphone. It is Toto, too, who delays Dorothy's return home after getting distracted by a cat – although they are eventually reunited.

In *The Wonderful Wizard of Oz* the creator of the thirteen Oz novels, L. Frank Baum, never specified Toto's breed, but wrote: 'He was a little black dog with long silky hair and small black eyes that twinkled merrily on either side of his funny, wee nose.' Toto was played in the film by

Terry, a female brindle Cairn terrier whose salary, $125 per week (equivalent to $2200 today), was more than that of many human actors in the film, and also more than most working Americans at the time.

U

UNDERDOGS

A powerful sense of hierarchy is essential to the dog world – although this is not fixed in perpetuity but can be tested and changed. As for human hierarchy, politics challenges the idea that this could ever be permanent. *The Oxford English Dictionary* thus defines 'underdog' as 'the beaten dog in a fight; the party overcome or worsted in a contest; one who is in a state of inferiority or subjection'. The *OED* further tells us that the word originated in the USA, giving an example from 1887 as an early UK usage. *Daily Telegraph* 30 April 1887: 'There is an indefinable expression in his face and figure of having been vanquished, of having succumbed, of having been "under-dog" as the saying is; while the *Daily Chronicle* on 26 March 1906 has 'I recall… many [situations] in which I started as under-dog and came out top-dog.'

V

VERSE FOR A CERTAIN DOG

Such glorious faith as fills your limpid eyes,
Dear little friend of mine, I never knew.
All-innocent are you, and yet all-wise.
(For Heaven's sake, stop worrying that shoe!)
You look about, and all you see is fair;
This mighty globe was made for you alone.
Of all the thunderous ages, you're the heir.
(Get off the pillow with that dirty bone!)

A skeptic world you face with steady gaze;
High in young pride you hold your noble head,
Gayly you meet the rush of roaring days.
(Must you eat puppy biscuit on the bed?)
Lancelike your courage, gleaming swift and strong,
Yours the white rapture of a winged soul,
Yours is a spirit like a Mayday song.
(God help you, if you break the goldfish bowl!)

'Whatever is, is good' – your gracious creed.
You wear your joy of living like a crown.
Love lights your simplest act, your every deed.

(Drop it, I tell you – put that kitten down!)
You are God's kindliest gift of all – a friend.
Your shining loyalty unflecked by doubt,
You ask but leave to follow to the end.
(Couldn't you wait until I took you out?)

Dorothy Parker (1893–1967)

VIVISECTION AND THE BROWN DOG

The visitor to Battersea Park who finds the narrow woodland path between the Buddhist stupa and the Old English Garden may chance upon a bronze statue on a plinth of a small dog, twisted in pain or humble supplication or both. A distressing inscription reads:

> In Memory of the Brown Terrier
> Dog Done to Death in the Laboratories
> of University College in February
> 1903 after having endured Vivisection
> extending over more than Two Months
> and having been handed over from
> one Vivisector to Another
> Till Death came to his Release.
>
> Also in Memory of the 232 dogs
> Vivisected at the same place during the year 1902.
>
> Men and Women of England
> how long shall these Things be?

On 2 February 1903, this nameless brown terrier cross was operated on, before an audience of 60 medical students, by Professor Starling and his brother-in-law William Bayliss, both of the Department of Physiology at University College London. The two men were considered 'compulsive experimenters': their researches on dogs would eventually lead to the discovery of hormones. In December 1902, the brown dog had had his abdomen cut open and his pancreatic duct ligated. For the following two months he lived in a cage. Then Bayliss used him again for two procedures in February, when two Swedish feminists were present, taking notes.

Outside the lecture room, and before the students arrived, according to testimony later given in court, Starling cut the dog open again to inspect the results of the previous surgery, which took about 45 minutes, after which he clamped the wound with forceps and handed the dog over to Bayliss. The latter cut a new opening in the dog's neck to expose the lingual nerves of the salivary glands, to which he attached electrodes. His aim was to stimulate the nerves electrically to demonstrate that salivation was independent of blood pressure. The dog was then carried to the lecture theatre, stretched on his back on an operating board, with his legs tied to it, his head clamped and his mouth muzzled. Bayliss stimulated the nerves for half an hour, but was unable to demonstrate his point. The dog was finally handed to a student, Henry Dale, a future Nobel laureate, who removed the dog's pancreas, then killed him with a knife through the heart.

According to Bayliss, the dog had earlier that day been given a morphine injection, and was further anaesthetised during the procedure with six fluid ounces of alcohol, chloroform and ether delivered from an anteroom to a tube in his trachea, via a hidden pipe. The two Swedish women who had gained access to the lecture theatre claimed, however, that the dog had arched his back and jerked his legs in what seemed like an effort to escape. When the experiment began, the dog continued to 'heave its abdomen' and to tremble, they said. They regarded his movements as 'violent and purposeful'. They also recorded that they had neither smelled any anaesthetic nor seen any apparatus delivering it.

An angry speech about this dog was given on 1 May 1903 to the annual meeting of the National Anti-Vivisection Society at St James's Hall, Piccadilly, attended by 2000 plus people. The lecturer accused the scientists of torture: 'If this is not torture, let Mr Bayliss and his friends... tell us in Heaven's name what torture is.' This issue was scarcely a new one. Robert Browning in 1870 had written a short satirical poem titled 'Tray' about a heroic dog who saves a life and is rewarded for his pains by vivisection. There were approximately 300 experiments on animals in the UK in 1875, an annual figure that had risen in 1903 to 19,084.

Prior to the experiment performed on the brown dog at UCL, the two Swedish women had visited the Pasteur Institute in Paris, a centre for animal experimentation, and were shocked by the rooms full of caged animals given diseases by the researchers. They founded the Swedish Anti-Vivisection Society before enrolling as students at the London School of Medicine for Women, a vivisection-free college with visiting arrangements at other London colleges, to train for their campaign. They attended in all some 100 lectures and demonstrations at King's and University College, including 50 experiments on live animals.

That July 1903 – and against legal advice – they published their anti-vivisection diary entitled *The Shambles of Science* where the word 'shambles' is used in its old-fashioned sense to mean slaughterhouse. One potentially slanderous chapter was called 'Fun'. This referred to the laughter they heard that February day in the lecture room both during the procedure and when the dog was finally killed.

Bayliss was outraged by this assault on his reputation and sued for libel. The 1876 Cruelty to Animals Act, which had made anaesthesia a legal requirement in vivisection, had also forbidden the use of the same animal in more than one single experiment. The terrier was vivisected twice. Bayliss nonetheless won his case and was awarded £2000 with £3000 costs.

It was a bitter blow to the two Swedish women but some prominent voices were raised in protest. In December 1903, Mark Twain, who opposed vivisection, published a pertinent short story, 'A Dog's Tale', in *Harper's*, written from the point of view of a dog whose puppy is experimented on and killed.

In 1997, journalist Peter Mason published a book – *The Brown Dog Affair* – telling of the turbulent and forgotten social history that followed: it has the apt and striking subtitle 'The Story of a Monument that Divided a Nation'. After the trial, the World League Against Vivisection raised £120 for a public memorial, and commissioned a bronze statue of the dog from sculptor Joseph Whitehead. The statue was unveiled on 15 September 1906 in front of a large crowd, with George Bernard Shaw among the speakers. The dog statue sat on a granite memorial stone housing a drinking fountain and trough for dogs and horses; and its inscription incriminating University College made it a strange cause célèbre and an incendiary flashpoint for years of social conflict.

London medical students soon instigated acts of disruption. The first came on 20 November 1907, when an undergraduate called William Howard Lister led a group enraged by the inscription across the Thames to attack the statue with a crowbar and sledgehammer. Ten were arrested and several fined £5. This triggered a further protest two days later: 1000 medical students marched along the Strand. Women's suffrage meetings were interrupted and the rioting reached its height on Tuesday, 10 December, when 100 medical students again tried to pull the memorial down. Street vendors sold handkerchiefs stamped with the date of the protest and the words: 'Brown Dog's inscription is a lie, and the statuette an insult to the London University'. A second group of students on the same day headed for central London, waving effigies of the Brown Dog, and were joined by a police escort and, briefly, a busker with bagpipes. A thousand marchers gathered around Nelson's Column, where ringleaders tried to make speeches, while students fought with 400 police on the ground, and fifteen mounted officers charged the crowd, scattering them into smaller groups and arresting the stragglers.

Over the following days and months, rioting broke out elsewhere and trade unionists, socialists, Marxists, liberals and suffragettes descended on Battersea to fight the medical students. The 'Brown Terrier Dog Done to Death' by the male scientific establishment united them all. Perhaps the iconography of vivisection struck a chord with suffragettes force-fed in prison.

Policing the statue now required six constables a day at a cost of £700 per year, and after questions were asked in the House of Commons about this growing expense, Battersea Council was asked to contribute to this sum. Some councillors suggested the statue be encased in a steel cage and surrounded by barbed wire.

Battersea Council tired of the controversy. A new Conservative council was elected in November 1909, amid talk of removing the statue. But there were protests in support of it, and the 500-strong Brown Dog Memorial Defense Committee was established. Twenty thousand people signed a petition, 1500 attended a rally in February 1910, and there were further demonstrations in central London and speeches in Hyde Park, with supporters wearing dog-masks.

These protests were to little avail. Before dawn on 10 March 1910, the statue was quietly removed by four council workmen, accompanied by 120 police officers. Nine days later 3000 anti-vivisectionists in Trafalgar Square demanded its return, but it was clear by then that Battersea Council had turned its back on the affair. The statue was first hidden in the borough surveyor's bicycle shed, then reportedly destroyed by a council blacksmith who melted it down. Anti-vivisectionists filed a High Court petition demanding its return; the case was dismissed in January 1911.

Over 75 years later, on 12 December 1985, the present memorial to the Brown Dog was unveiled in Battersea Park behind the Pump House. Commissioned by anti-vivisectionists and created by sculptor Nicola Hicks, the new dog, mounted on a five-foot-high plinth, is based on Hicks's own terrier, Brock. Echoing the fate of the previous memorial, the new dog was moved into storage in 1992 by the Conservative Borough of Wandsworth, purportedly as part of a park renovation scheme. Anti-vivisectionists, suspicious of this explanation, campaigned for its return and it was reinstated in 1994, in a more secluded spot.

One plaque on the new Brown Dog's plinth brings the story up-to-date: 'Animal experimentation is one of the greatest moral issues of our time and should have no place in a civilised society... During 1984, 3,497,335 experiments were performed on live animals [in the UK]. Today, animals are burned, blinded, irradiated, poisoned and subjected to countless other horrifyingly cruel experiments in Great Britain.'

W

WALKING THE DOG

Two universes mosey down the street
Connected by love and a leash and nothing else.
Mostly I look at lamplight through the leaves
While he mooches along with tail up and snout down,
Getting a secret knowledge through the nose
Almost entirely hidden from my sight.

We stand while he's enraptured by a bush
Till I can't stand our standing any more
And haul him off; for our relationship
Is patience balancing to this side tug
And that side drag; a pair of symbionts
Contented not to think each other's thoughts.

What else we have in common's what he taught,
Our interest in shit. We know its every state
From steaming fresh through stink to nature's way
Of sluicing it downstreet dissolved in rain
Or drying it to dust that blows away.
We move along the street inspecting shit.

His sense of it is keener far than mine,
And only when he finds the place precise
He signifies by sniffing urgently
And circles thrice about, and squats, and shits,
Whereon we both with dignity walk home
And just to show who's master I write the poem.

Howard Nemerov (1920–91)

WOLF-DOG HYBRIDS

A conventional narrative claims that human beings tamed dogs between 10,000 and 20,000 years ago; a curious and provocative counter-narrative points out that dogs may have seduced and tamed us to provide them for life with shelter, care and food. All dogs descend from wolves, and all varieties of dog today can still mate and hybridise with wolves, with whom they share 98.8% of their DNA. Yet wolves are even now sometimes feared and demonised, while dogs are cherished and loved. Roger Grenier (see page 17) maintains that if a wolf cub less than six weeks old is brought up by a human being, it will be fully domesticated and behave exactly like a dog; and conversely that a puppy raised 'wild' without human contact for the first three months of life quickly becomes untameable and will remain completely wild…

THE WOODMAN'S DOG

Forth goes the woodman, leaving unconcerned
The cheerful haunts of men – to wield the axe
And drive the wedge in yonder forest drear,
From morn to eve his solitary task.
Shaggy and lean and shrewd with pointed ears,
And tail cropped short, half lurcher and half cur,
His dog attends him. Close behind his heel
Now creeps he slow; and now, with many a frisk
Wide-scampering, snatches up the drifted snow
With ivory teeth, or ploughs it with his snout;
Then shakes his powdered coat, and barks for joy.

From 'The Task' Book V, William Cowper
(1731–1800)

Y

YOFI AND FREUD

Late in his life, Freud discovered the uses of dogs. His daughter Anna recalled his assertion that 'dogs love their friends and bite their enemies'; this contrasted with men who are 'incapable of pure love and must at all times mix love and hate in their object relations'. In a letter to his patron Marie Bonaparte, he explained that dogs provide 'affection without ambivalence, the simplicity of a life free from the almost unbearable conflicts of civilisation, the beauty of an existence complete in itself.' Freud also valued in his dogs their gracefulness, devotion and fidelity.

The first dog to live at Freud's apartment on the Berggasse in Vienna was a German shepherd named Wolf. Freud gave him to Anna in 1925 to protect her on long walks. But Wolf's services extended on one occasion to biting Freud's colleague and future biographer Ernest Jones. Freud felt that Jones deserved it. In 1928, Freud acquired a dog of his own, Lün Yug, a chow who was run over by a train the following summer when only fifteen months old. Freud, dejected, could not consider getting a replacement until the following spring, when he acquired

Lün Yug's sister Yofi, who would become his cherished pet for the next seven years.

'Yofi' is the Hebrew word for 'beauty'; she accompanied Freud on his walks and at mealtimes, and was at his side even in his office with its famed couch. The dog's presence apparently helped reduce tension in the room: patients would open up more when Yofi was there. Freud's housekeeper remembered Freud claiming that Yofi – non-judgmental and a focused and silent observer – had keen insight, sitting closer to the couch and making herself available for petting if a patient was anxious or depressed. And Freud could always tell when the hour was up because Yofi became restless, yawning and wandering about to signal that the session was over.

Freud often mentions Yofi in his diaries, noting such details as her general health, her stays at kennels and the unhappy fates of her litters: of her first, only one survived before succumbing to distemper. Yofi ate part of her second litter and the puppy Freud had designated for the partner of one of his patients bit someone and had to be put down. Freud wrote: 'Often when stroking Yofi, I have caught myself humming a melody which, unmusical as I am, I can't help recognising as the aria from *Don Giovanni*: A bond of friendship unites us both...' '*O heiliges Band der Freundschaft treuer Brüder*' does not come from *Don Giovanni*, though it is by Mozart.

When Yofi died after a complicated operation to remove some ovarian cysts, Freud mourned her, writing: 'One cannot easily get over seven years of intimacy.'

Ernest Jones observed that Freud now understood that he couldn't live without a dog. Yofi had originally come into the household with another, gentler chow, Lün, (named after Lün Yug) but she had to be given away to friends because the two could not get on. The day after Yofi's death, Lün returned to Freud and travelled with him from Vienna to London during the summer of 1938. Upon arriving in Dover, Lün was taken from him and placed in quarantine kennels at Ladbroke Grove. Five days later, after Freud had settled into his new house, he ventured out to visit her. He was 82, tired and frail, and already very sick with oral cancer. Lün leapt to meet him and Freud played with her and talked to her, using many little terms of endearment, for an hour. After six months, Lün came home.

In the last days of Freud's illness, it pained him that Lün avoided him, probably because of his necrotic jaw. In September 1939, he made the decision to end his life with an overdose of morphine, approaching his end with characteristic stoicism. Lün was given away.

YOKO

All today I lie in the bottom of the wardrobe
feeling low but sometimes getting up
to moodily lumber across rooms
and lap from the toilet bowl, it is so sultry
and then I hear the noise of firecrackers again
all New York is jaggedy with firecrackers today
and I go back to the wardrobe gloomy
trying to void my mind of them.
I am confused, I feel loose and unfitted.

At last deep in the stairwell I hear a tread,
it is him, my leader, my love.
I run to the door and listen to his approach.
Now I can smell him, what a good man he is,
I love it when he has the sweat of work on him,
as he enters I yodel with happiness,
I throw my body up against his, I try to lick his lips,
I care about him more than anything.

After we eat we go for a walk to the piers.
I leap into the standing warmth, I plunge into

the combination of old and new smells.
Here on a garbage can at the bottom, so interesting,
what sister or brother I wonder left this message I sniff.
I too piss there, and go on.
Here a hydrant there a pole
here's a smell I left yesterday, well that's disappointing
but I piss there anyway, and go on.

I investigate so much that in the end
it is for form's sake only, only a drop comes out.

I investigate tar and rotten sandwiches, everything, and go on.

And here a dried old turd, so interesting
so old, so dry, yet so subtle and mellow.
I can place it finely, I really appreciate it,
a gold distant smell like packed autumn leaves in winter
reminding me how what is rich and fierce when excreted
becomes weathered and mild
                                        but always interesting
and reminding me of what I have to do.

My leader looks on and expresses his approval.

I sniff it well and later I sniff the air well
a wind is meeting us after the close July day
rain is getting near too but first the wind.
Joy, joy,
being outside with you, active, investigating it all,

with bowels emptied, feeling your approval
and then running on, the big fleet Yoko,
my body in its excellent black coat never lets me down,
returning to you (as I always will, you know that)
and now
          filling myself out with myself, no longer confused,
my panting pushing apart my black lips, but unmoving,
I stand with you braced against the wind.

Thom Gunn (1929–2004)

ACKNOWLEDGMENTS

I am grateful that copyright permission was generously and imaginatively granted – gratis – by Bloodaxe Books (www.bloodaxebooks.com) to reproduce W.S. Merwin's 'Dog Dreaming' from his *Selected Poems* (2007) and granted by Chicago University Press to reproduce Howard Nemerov's 'Walking the Dog'.

Permission to quote has otherwise been sought as follows: C. Day Lewis, 'Sheepdog Trials in Hyde Park'; William Dickey's 'Hope' from Wesleyan University Press; Robert Graves' 'Escape' from Random House; Thom Gunn's 'Yoko' from Faber; Dorothy Parker's 'Verse for a Certain Dog' from Random House; Siegfried Sassoon's 'Man and Dog' from the Barbara Levy Agency.

Dr Harriet Harvey Wood, Tony Morris and Aurea Carpenter each had helpful suggestions. The following list comprises some published sources to which I am particularly indebted.

INTRODUCTION

Ciuaru, Carmela, *Dog Poems* (2003).

Devlin, Polly on Elizabeth M. Thomas, *The Independent*, 22 May 1994. www.independent.co.uk/arts-entertainment/book-review-absolutely-mad-about-barking-the-hidden-life-of-dogs-elizabeth-marshall-thomas-1437669.html

Grenier, Roger, *Les larmes d'Ulysse* (1998), tr. Alice Kaplan, *The Difficulty of Being a Dog* (2002).

Hastings, Max on Carmela Ciuaru's *Dog Poems*. www.telegraph.co.uk/culture/books/3608445/Poetic-dog-licence.html

Thomas, Elizabeth M., *The Hidden Life of Dogs* (1994).

ARGOS

Homer, *Odyssey* tr. Stanley Lombardo (2000).

THE CARPACCIO DOG

Morris, Jan, *Carpaccio* (2014).

CHAUCER

Canterbury Tales, tr. Neville Coghill (1951).

DICKENS'S DIOGENES AND OTHER DOGS

Gray, Beryl, *The Dog in the Dickensian Imagination* (2014) and *Carlyle Studies Annual* no 22, Spring 2006, pp 181-212.

FLUSH AND VIRGINIA WOOLF

Adams, Maureen, *Shaggy Muses: The Dogs Who Inspired Virginia Woolf, Emily Dickinson, Elizabeth Barrett Browning, Edith Wharton and Emily Bronte* (2007).

GREYFRIARS BOBBY

'Greyfriars Bobby was just a Victorian publicity stunt, claims academic', *The Telegraph*, 3 August 2011. www.telegraph.co.uk/news/newstopics/howaboutthat/8678875/Greyfriars-Bobby-was-just-a-Victorian-publicity-stunt-claims-academic.html;

Bondeson, Jan, *Greyfriars Bobby: The Most Faithful Dog in the World* (2011).

Brassey, Richard, *Greyfriars Bobby The Most Famous Dog in Scotland* (2010).

Macgregor, Forbes, *Greyfriars Bobby: The Real Story at Last* (1998).

Velten, Hannah. www.roundthewatertrough.wordpress.com/2014/02/03/greyfriars-bobby-a-shaggy-dog-story/

LAIKA

Batchelor, Tom, 'Laika at 60: What happens to all the dogs, monkeys and mice sent into space?', *The Independent*, 3 November 2017. www.independent.co.uk/news/science/laiki-60-anniversary-russia-space-dog-what-happens-to-animals-sent-into-orbit-a8036411.html

MARY QUEEN OF SCOTS

www.graceelliot-author.blogspot.com/2014/04/mary-queen-of-scots-and-her-dogs.html

NERO AND JANE WELSH CARLYLE

Ashton, Rosemary, *Thomas and Jane Carlyle: Portrait of a Marriage* (2002).

Chamberlain, Kathy, *Jane Welsh Carlyle and her Victorian World* (2017).

NIPPER

'Inventing Entertainment: The Early Motion Pictures and Sound Recordings of the Edison Companies', Library of Congress. www.loc.gov/collections/edison-company-motion-pictures-and-sound-recordings/articles-and-essays/history-of-edison-sound-re

POLLY AND DARWIN

Allan Feller, David, 'Darwin the Dog Lover', Forbes Magazine, 2009. www.forbes.com/2009/02/05/dogs-hunting-cambridge-university-opinions-darwin09_0205_david_allen_feller.html#341c87ad36f3

National Pure Breed Dog Day. www.nationalpurebreddogday.com/darwins-dogs/

Darwin Correspondence Project, Cambridge University Library. www.darwinproject.ac.uk/commentary/life-sciences/darwin-and-vivisection

QUEENIE AND J.R. ACKERLEY

Ackerley, J.R., *My Dog Tulip* (1956).

SHAKESPEARE

Stephen Greenblatt, 'A Great Dane Goes to the Dogs,' *New York Review of Books*, March 26, 2009, and ensuing correspondence May 14, 2009. Caroline Spurgeon, *Shakespeare's Imagery, and what it tells us* (1935).

TITANIC

Eveleth, Rose, 'The definitive guide to the dogs on the